U0461542

跨境电商物流
供应链的管理和优化
（中英文）

谢桂梅　张玲 ◎ 著

MANAGEMENT AND OPTIMIZATION
OF CROSS-BORDER E-COMMERCE
LOGISTICS AND SUPPLY CHAIN
(CHINESE AND ENGLISH)

知识产权出版社
全国百佳图书出版单位
—北京—

图书在版编目（CIP）数据

跨境电商物流供应链的管理和优化：汉、英/谢桂梅，张玲著．—北京：知识产权出版社，2024.4

ISBN 978－7－5130－9045－2

Ⅰ．①跨…　Ⅱ．①谢…②张…　Ⅲ．①电子商务—物流管理—供应链管理—研究—汉、英　Ⅳ．①F713.365.1

中国国家版本馆 CIP 数据核字（2023）第 226979 号

责任编辑：国晓健　　　　　　　　　责任校对：谷　洋
封面设计：臧　磊　　　　　　　　　责任印制：孙婷婷

跨境电商物流供应链的管理和优化（中英文）

Management and Optimization of Cross-border E-commerce Logistics and Supply Chain (Chinese and English)

谢桂梅　张　玲　著

出版发行：知识产权出版社 有限责任公司	网　　址：http://www.ipph.cn
社　　址：北京市海淀区气象路 50 号院	邮　　编：100081
责编电话：010－82000860 转 8385	责编邮箱：anxuchuban@126.com
发行电话：010－82000860 转 8101/8102	发行传真：010－82000893/82005070/82000270
印　　刷：北京九州迅驰传媒文化有限公司	经　　销：新华书店、各大网上书店及相关专业书店
开　　本：787mm×1092mm　1/16	印　　张：14.25
版　　次：2024 年 4 月第 1 版	印　　次：2024 年 4 月第 1 次印刷
字　　数：282 千字	定　　价：86.00 元
ISBN 978－7－5130－9045－2	

写在前面的话

跨境电商物流供应链关系到跨境电商产业的发展，关系到我国对外贸易的顺利进行，进而影响我国的"双循环"战略和中国经济的持续健康发展。在国际政治、经济、社会形势的大局下，审视国内外物流和供应链发展现状和研究成果，认清形势，迎接挑战，是学界义不容辞的责任。本书综述了我国跨境电商物流供应链的最新研究成果，针对物流供应链发展中面临的挑战和风险，提出一定的优化策略，助力我国经济发展。

本书在编写过程中，得到何明珂教授和杜志平教授的指导和帮助，以及北京物资学院外语学院王淑花院长和任丽丽副院长的鼓励和支持，在此一并感谢。两位作者进行了大量阅读和深入探讨，表述尽量客观、全面。限于才疏学浅，不当之处恳请斧正。

Forword

Cross-border E-commerce(CBEC) logistics and supply chain is closely connected with the development of Cross-border E-commerce industry and foreign trade, and then affects China's dual economic circulation strategy and the sustainable and healthy development of China's economy. In view of the current international politics, economy and social situation, we find that it is imperative for academic circles to reexamine the current status and research achievements home and abroad in logistics and supply chain, recognize the situation, and embrace the challenges. This research synthesizes the latest research findings of China's Cross-border E-commerce logistics and supply chain, and proposes certain optimization strategies to the challenges and risks in its development to facilitate the growth of China's economy.

In the process of writing this book, we received the guidance and assistance from Prof. He Mingke and Prof. Du Zhiping, as well as encouragement and support from the Dean Wang Shuhua and Vice Dean Ren Lili of the School of Foreign Languages and Cultures of Beijing Wuzi University. We really appreciate that We have read extensively, discussed deeply, and tried our best to express ideas in an objective and comprehensive approach. Due to our limited insights of this issue, we are willing to invite any comments from our readers.

前　言

　　当前，跨境电商已成为中国外贸的新动力、新源泉和中国经济的新增长点。据海关统计，我国跨境电商进出口规模 5 年来（2017—2022）扩大近 10 倍，跨境电商占外贸的比重由 2015 年的不到 1% 增长到 2021 年的 4.9%。① 这一成绩不仅受益于中央政府和地方政府出台的一系列政策的红利和创新实践，也得益于经济全球化的宏观大环境。在已形成的跨境电商生态系统中，跨境电商平台、跨境物流、跨境支付、信息系统、基础设施、国际政治、经济制度、文化环境等因素互相配合，共同打造跨境电商生态系统，维持跨境电商的顺畅发展。在跨境电商发展的短短二十多年（2000 年以来）历史中，跨境物流得到了一定发展，同时也成了跨境电商发展的"痛点"：物流和商流的成本、效率和服务极大地制约着跨境电商的发展。物流成本的居高不下、物流运输和配送的低效率不能满足跨境电商商家、跨境平台和国外消费者的要求，极大地影响了消费者体验，制约着跨境电商产业和物流供应链产业的发展。

　　2022 年以来，我国加快建设制造强国、质量强国、航天强国、交通强国、网络强国、数字中国，需要强大的物流供应链的支撑。党的二十大报告强调了物流的重要性以及降低物流成本的迫切需求："……加快发展物联网，建设高效顺畅的流通体系，降低物流成本。"跨境电商和跨境物流是中国经济双循环格局的重要力量。21 世纪 20 年代以来，地缘政治冲突、

---

① 智通财经. 商务部：中国跨境电商 5 年增长将近 10 倍 今年一季度仍然继续保持高速增长势头［EB/OL］. （2023 - 11 - 22）［2023 - 04 - 23］. https：//baijiahao. baidu. com/s?id = 17639384 15309271400&wfr = spider&for = pc.

反全球化浪潮、中美贸易摩擦、新冠疫情等一系列不利于跨境电商的因素不断增多，跨境物流供应链受到了较大的影响，发展出现了较大的波动。因此，对跨境电商物流供应链的管理和优化进行研究有着深刻的现实意义和理论意义。

本书以跨境电商为出发点，结合当前跨境物流供应链发展的现状，探讨跨境电商物流供应链的发展方向和面临的挑战，并对其管理和优化提出自己的观点。本书的创新之处在于，从跨境电商生态系统出发，构建跨境物流供应链生态系统，从生态系统角度探讨微观和宏观的影响因素和优化策略。微观层面包括跨境电商平台、跨境物流企业（第三方物流、第四方物流、物流联盟、外综服企业、海外仓）的管理和优化、风险和应对等。宏观层面的考量主要借助 PESTEL 分析模型，分析 6 大宏观环境因素对跨境电商物流供应链的影响，尤其是制度距离和文化距离等对跨境电商物流供应链可持续长远发展的重要影响，以整合思维和集成思维为理念引导，提出相应的管理和优化建议。海外仓被认为是解决物流供应链困境的焦点，基于此，本书第 5 章以部分公司为例，详细探讨物流供应链优化中的风险、挑战和优化。

Preface

At present, Cross-border E-commerce has become a new driving force and source of China's foreign trade and a new growth point for China's economy. According to customs statistics, China's Cross-border E-commerce import and export volume has increased nearly 10 times in the past five years since 2017, and the percentage of Cross-border E-commerce in proportion to China's whole foreign trade had increased from less than 1% in 2015 to 4. 9% in 2021. [1] The great achievement not only benefited from the dividends and innovative practices of a series of policies issued by the central and local governments, but also benefited from economic globalization. In a well-functioned Cross-border E-commerce ecosystem (including Cross-border E-commerce platform, Cross-border logistics, Cross-border payment, information system, infrastructure, international politics, economic system, cultural environment, etc.), all factors work together to create an ecosystem and maintain the smooth development of Cross-border E-commerce. In the 20-plus years' history of Cross-border E-commerce since 2000, Cross-border logistics has seen a progress, and has also become a "pain point" of Cross-border E-commerce development: the cost, efficiency and service of logistics and business flow have greatly hindered the development of Cross-border E-com-

---

[1] Zhitongcaijing. Ministry of Commerce: China's Cross-border E-commerce has grown nearly 10 times in 5 years and continues to maintain a high-speed growth momentum in the first quarter of this year [EB/OL]. (2023 - 11 - 22) [2023 - 04 - 23]. https://baijiahao. baidu. com/s? id = 17639384153 09271400&wfr = spider&for = pc.

merce. The high cost of logistics and the low efficiency of logistics transportation and distribution cannot meet the requirements of Cross-border E-commerce sellers, Cross-border platforms and foreign consumers, which greatly affect consumer experience and restrict the development of the Cross-border E-commerce industry and the logistics and supply chain industry.

Since the year of 2022, China has been moving faster to boost its strength in manufacturing, product quality, aerospace, transportation, cyberspace, and digital development, which asks for the support of a strong logistics and supply chain. *The Report to the 20th National Congress of the Communist Party of China* (CPC) stressed the importance of logistics and the urgent need to reduce the cost of logistics: . . . *accelerate development of the Internet of Things and build an efficient and smooth logistics system to help cut distribution costs.* Cross-border E-commerce and Cross-border logistics are important forces in the dual circulation of China's economy. However, since the year of 2020, a series of factors, such as geopolitical conflict, anti-globalization wave, Sino-US trade friction, COVID-19, etc. , have emerged one after another which affected cross-border logistics and supply chain and aroused great fluctuation. Hence, the research on the management and optimization of Cross-border E-commerce logistics and supply chain has profound practical and theoretical significance.

Based on the current situation of Cross-border logistics and supply chain, this book starts with Cross-border E-commerce, discusses the development direction and challenges of Cross-border E-commerce logistics and supply chain, and puts forward views on the management and optimization of logistics and supply chain. The innovation of this book is to build a Cross-border logistics and supply chain ecosystem from the perspective of Cross-border E-commerce ecosystem, and explore micro-level and macro-level factors and optimization strategies. At the micro-level, suggestions such as the management and optimization of Cross-border E-commerce platforms, and Cross-border logistics enterprises (the third party logistics, the fourth party logistics, logistics alliances, foreign comprehensive service enterprises, and overseas warehouses), risk and response are presented. Overseas warehouse is considered to be a focus of solving the logistics and supply chain dilemma. Macroscopic considerations mainly rely on the PESTEL analysis model to analyze the impact of six macro factors on the Cross-border E-commerce logistics and supply chain, especially the institutional distance and cultural distance, which are important forces for the sustainable long-term development of Cross-border E-commerce logistics and supply chain. All the corresponding management and optimization suggestions are put forward in this book within the framework of integrative thinking pattern. Based on this fact, Chapter 5 takes a few companies as examples to discuss the risks, challenges and optimization in the logistics and supply chain in detail.

目　录

Contents

第1章　跨境电商及物流供应链生态系统

本章聚焦跨境电商、跨境电商生态系统、跨境电商物流供应链的参与主体、跨境电商物流供应链系统，以及跨境电商与物流供应链的协同。

1.1　跨境电商

1.1.1　跨境电商的定义

跨境电商有广义和狭义之分。广义的跨境电商泛指一切利用电子方式进行的商业活动，包括数据传输、合同的谈判和签署、票据的传输、跨境金融、跨境物流等活动。狭义的跨境电商多指由跨境电商平台主导，以跨境 B2B、B2C、C2C 模式为主的商业买卖活动，尤其指跨境零售活动。商流、物流、资金流、信息流构成跨境电商的四个维度。根据百度百科的解释，跨境电商是指分属不同关境的交易主体，通过电子商务平台达成交易、进行支付结算，并通过跨境物流送达商品、完成交易的电子商务平台和在线交易平台。这一从交易流程定义的跨境电商是狭义的跨境电商，也是本书研究的对象。它是传统国际贸易网络化、电子化的衍生和发展，借助互联网、信息通信技术和现代物流的便利，以此为基础，以国际商务为核心，改变传统销售、购物渠道，打破国家与地区间有形或无形的界限，减少面对面的现场沟通等中间环节，节约传统交易成本，因而在世界范围内迅猛发展，成为全球国际贸易的新业态，也成为中国经济的新增长动力。

传统的跨境贸易流程为：国内制造企业—国内出口商—国外进口商—批发商—零售商—消费者。产品从制造企业到消费者之间经历多层中间商，渠道成本高昂。而跨境电子商务的发展大大压缩了中间环节，国内企业直接对接外国零售商甚至消费者，扁平化的出口贸易链条降低了渠道成本，提高了供应链效率。我国跨境电商进出口规模 2017 年至 2022 年增长近 10 倍。跨境电商占外贸的比重由 2015 年的不到 1% 增长到 2021 年的 4.9%，成为中国经济新的增长点。①

跨境电子商务有力地推动了全球经济的一体化和贸易的全球化，不仅打破了国家物理边界，使国际贸易走向无国界贸易，同时也引发了世界经济贸易结构、模式的巨大变革。对个人、企业、产业、国家、世界经济格局来说，跨境电子商务构建的开放、多维、立体的多边经贸合作模式，极大地拓宽了生产者和消费者进入国际市场的路径，有利于世界范围内物流供应链的发展，提升了世界范围内资源的优化配置，使企业之间达到互利共赢。消费者可以便捷地获取商品信息，买到物美价廉的商品。企业可以面对更多的客户群体，来自世界的消费者让产品有更大的市场，同时为消费者提供更好的服务。对国家来说，一国的生产制造能力能得到充分发挥，规模经济效应更加明显，产业链条不仅可以从国内延伸到国外，还可以带动相关产业（如制造业、物流、支付、信息技术、大数据、云计算、区块链等）及产业集群的发展，提升一国的工业生产制造能力，促进经贸双方经济的发展，创造更多的价值和效益，为世界带来更多的福利。

---

① 智通财经. 商务部：中国跨境电商 5 年增长将近 10 倍. 今年一季度仍然继续保持高速增长势头［EB/OL］. （2023 - 04 - 23）［2023 - 11 - 22］. https：//baijiahao. baidu. com/s？id = 1763938415309271400 & wfr = spider&for = pc.

1.1.2　跨境电商的参与主体

从微观来看，跨境电商是一个复杂的网络体系，也是一个复杂的产业生态系统，其中参与者众多，无论是进口还是出口，核心参与者首先是各类跨境电商平台，其他参与主体包括：生产商、制造商企业，消费者，支付平台企业（金融机构，包括银行、外汇平台、第三方支付企业等），跨境物流商及平台（包括货运代理、第三方物流、第四方物流、跨境物流联盟等），政府部门（如海关、商检等）、行业协会、技术支撑企业（如通信服务机构、信息技术机构、网络平台构建企业等）、跨境营销相关企业等，如图 1-1 所示。

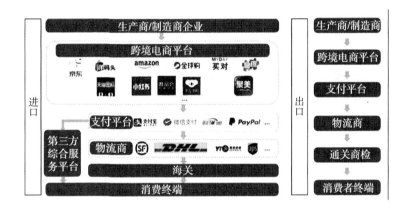

图 1-1　跨境电商参与主体（微观）

从宏观来看，跨境电商属于国际贸易，是商品跨越国境的交易行为，涉及至少两个国家的经贸规则、政治关系、经济发展水平、社会文化、风俗习惯，还受国际法规（如知识产权协议、隐私保护、数据传输协议等）或区域组织规则等制约。各参与主体相互作用，共同维护跨境电商生态环境的良好发展。跨境电商的各个环节像链条一样紧密相连，无论哪一环节出现波动，都会影响到相关环节，并随着链条运行被逐渐放大，从而影响整个跨境电商的运行。

1.2 跨境电商生态系统

如前所述，跨境电商以跨境电商平台为核心，以多方交易者和服务提供者以及监管者为参与主体，构成跨境电商生态系统。不少学者依据不同的侧重点，从不同的角度对跨境电商生态系统进行了定义和研究。跨境电商生态系统的构建经历了一个从平面化到立体化的过程，生态系统的构成从最初的三层次生态（核心层—支撑层—技术服务层），到中期的四层次生态（核心物种—关键物种—支持物种—外部环境），到目前的五层结构（核心物种—关键物种—支持物种—外围寄生物种—外部环境），跨境电商生态系统的结构和功能逐渐细化。

1.2.1 文献回顾

张薇（2016）基于平台战略的视角，运用平台商业模式理论布局我国跨境电商生态系统，如图1-2所示。她强调网络和信息技术等在跨境电商生态系统中的重要作用，认为跨境电商生态系统由核心层、支撑层和技术服务层构成。该理论中的核心层由跨境电商平台及平台上的买卖双方构成；支撑层由物流服务商、金融服务商、互联网服务提供商及它们相应的信息服务平台构成；技术服务层提供各种大数据服务、云计算服务，主要由平台运营服务提供商、软件服务提供商、营销服务提供商等完成。整个系统中信息数据无缝传输，维持整个系统的运转。该生态系统符合"互联网＋"时代外贸企业发展和竞争的需要。该研究结论认为，利用平台理论构建跨境电商生态系统能够实现信息共享，加强相关企业间的联系，提高工作效率，最终实现整个生态系统的协同发展。

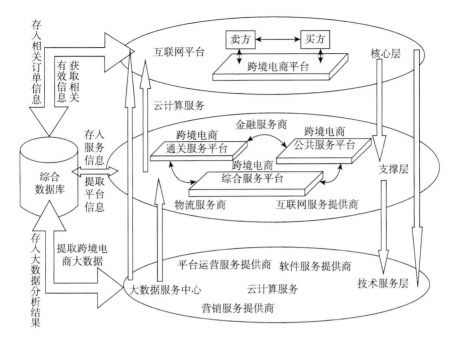

图 1-2 跨境电商生态系统（张薇，2016）

熊励、叶凯雯（2020）结合跨境电子商务按时间制定的政策，认为跨境电商生态系统包括三层：核心层为跨境电商活动群落，包括供应商、消费者以及跨境电商平台，该层形成于探索开拓期（2007 年前）。随着行业的发展，核心层周围的支持层得到了发展，包括提供公共服务与实施监管的支撑群落（政府部门）和提供报关、物流、支付等服务的服务群落（公服平台）。支撑群落较为特殊，既对服务群落产生制约，也对活动群落进行规范，并且能参与跨境电商政策的制定与实施。最外层为宏观因素即环境层，包括经济、社会和技术环境等。政策的制定过程也是跨境电商生态系统发展的过程。

张夏恒、郭海玲（2016）引入物种的概念来探讨跨境物流供应链生态系统。他们认为，跨境电商生态系统由 5 个物种构成：支持物种、核心物种、关键物种、寄生物种以及环境物种，如图 1-3 所示。核心物种为跨境电商平台，跨境电商平台也是信息流的一个重要节点；依靠平台进行连接的消费者和生产商构成关键物种；与物流和资金流紧密相关的物流企业和跨境支付企业等为支持物种；网络营销企业和各类广告、咨询服务机构，各类技术支持企业等为寄生物种；企业的内部环境和社会外部环境构成了环境因素。5 个物种相互配合，完成商流的运转。以此为基础，跨境电商生态系统各物种间相互协同，尤其是跨境电商和跨境物流供应链的协同是跨境电商发展的重中之重。

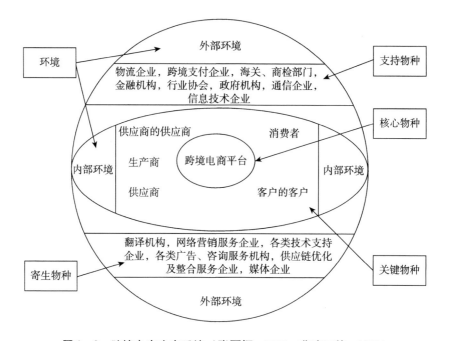

图 1-3　跨境电商生态系统（张夏恒，2016；曹武军等，2019）

曹武军等（2019）借鉴了上述跨境电商生态系统框架，强调了其整体性和系统性，具有一定的整合性思维。他们认为，跨境电商生态系统是互联网条件下以跨境电商平台为核心，由完成跨境电商平台商品交易的相关物种构成的有机整体。与跨境电子商务活动相关的个体、企业、组织或机构构成了该系统的物种，跨境电子商务平台为交流与沟通的媒介和渠道，各物种形成自己的生态位，它们之间通过各种形式进行优势互补、资源共享，实现物种间及物种与环境间动态的商品、资金、物流及信息的流动、沟通、分享与循环。

上述生态系统论都强调了跨境电商平台的核心作用，在这一点上，前述研究者都取得了一致观点。但在跨境物流的地位上，研究各有分歧，如张夏恒（2016）认为跨境物流是支持物种。实际业务操作中，跨境物流作为跨境电商发展中的一个关键环节，与跨境电商休戚相关。跨境物流的业务取决于跨境电商产业的发展，而跨境电商的发展必须依赖高效的物流系统，良好的跨境物流是跨境电商发展的基础和保证，二者的协调发展不但能促进两个产业各自的发展，也能使两个产业融合获得更好的发展。实业界和学术界都对跨境电商与物流供应链协同发展持一致观点（付帅帅等，2021；张夏恒，2016；张夏恒、郭海玲，2016；王宇楠，2022；米岩，2022；林子青，2020；杜志平、区钰贤，2020；韩玲冰等，2018；杨子等，2018；祁飞，2020），并进行了不少相关研究，提出了一系列建议和应对措施。

现实情况表明，尤其是 2020 年新型冠状病毒感染疫情以来，跨境物流先后经历了供应链断裂和恢复的剧烈波动，如 2022 年中国到美国西部海运集装箱单价大幅跳水，疫情期间从 2 万美元报价到低于 2 千美元报价[①]，价格不及 2020 年高峰时的 1/10，给跨境物流运输企业和电商企业等带来巨大的损失。全球经济衰退、地缘政治、碳达峰和碳中和的环境考虑等因素导致关税增加、规则更复杂。中美贸易摩擦，后疫情时代的消费心理，国际贸易规则的变化，区域经济的盛行，对数据的收集和传输的担忧，个人隐私保护，以及劳工和道德问题的考量等，使跨境电商发展的外部环境发生了巨大的变化。外部环境在跨境电商发展中的重要性越来越大。跨境物流作为跨境电商的关键支持力量，其发展也越来越受制于国际环境的变化。因此，在跨境电商发展的生态系统中，PESTEL 各因素也成为越来越重要的决定因素。

1.2.2　基于 PESTEL 理论的跨境电商生态系统

基于现实中环境因素的重要性，本章节借鉴 PESTEL 理论来分析跨境

---

① 20000 美元→1800 美元！美西运费已缩水 9/10，船只仅 3/4 满载率！跨大西洋航线也疲软［EB/OL］.（2022 - 10 - 13）［2023 - 1 - 18］. https：//business. sohu. com/a/592481307_121123842.

电商以及物流供应链。PESTEL 分析模型也叫大环境分析模型，是宏观环境分析的有效工具，不仅能分析外部环境，而且能识别一切对系统有冲击作用的力量。该模型有 6 大宏观因素：政治因素（Political）、经济因素（Economic）、社会因素（Social）、技术因素（Technological）、环境因素（Environmental）和法律因素（Legal）。根据以往的研究，多数学者认为信息系统、互联网等技术因素与跨境电商和物流紧密相关，技术因素构成了跨境电商生态的技术基础。这里的技术因素指代技术进步的大趋势，区别于个体公司的技术创新和应用。因此，跨境电商的宏观环境由 PESTEL 6 个因素构成。

微观来看，一方面，跨境电商和跨境物流之间发展不协调，已经成为跨境电商发展的"痛点"。另一方面，跨境电商生态系统必须考虑更多的外部环境因素，才能更好地促进跨境电商微观层面的长期、稳定发展。因此，本书从跨境电商以及跨境电商物流供应链长期、稳定、良性发展的角度出发，构建跨境电商生态系统（图 1-4），并在此基础上分析跨境电商物流供应链生态系统，以及其发展、挑战、管理和优化。

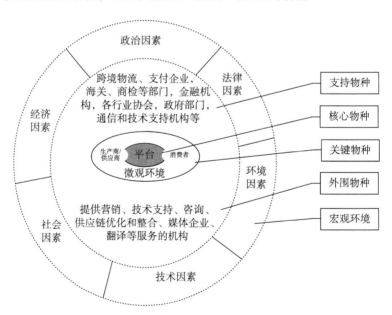

图 1-4　PESTEL 理论支撑的跨境电商生态系统

1.2.2.1　微观环境因素

（1）核心物种

跨境电子商务平台是现代信息技术下的独创性伟大应用，是跨境电商生态系统中的核心物种。它是整个跨境电子商务生态系统的原点，是生态系统中的首席资源分配者和启动者。系统通过商品交易平台，提供交易信息、收集交易信息，监督和管理交易流程，提供支付、售后等服务，承担着整个跨境电子商务生态系统的资源整合和协调的作用。

（2）关键物种

跨境电子商品买卖交易的直接交易主体构成了关键物种：跨境商品交易的买方和卖方。卖方向上可以延伸到供应商、生产商、投资商以及供应商的供应商，买方向下可以延伸至客户以及客户的客户等。这些物种是跨境电子商务生态系统里其他物种服务的对象。对跨境物流而言，也是物流供应链的直接服务对象。

（3）支持物种

支持物种是与跨境电子商务关系最为紧密的物种，具体指支持跨境电商交易的相关企业、部门或机构，包括跨境支付企业、跨境物流企业、海关部门、商检部门、金融机构、各行业协会、相关政府部门、通信和技术支持机构等。支持物种，顾名思义，是围绕核心物种与关键物种开展支持活动，支撑跨境电子商务生态系统最低限度正常运行的物种。跨境物流供应链作为关键支持物种，是本书的研究对象，也是整个跨境电商的"痛点"。

（4）外围物种

在跨境电子商务交易中提供增值服务的群体，包括跨境网络营销服务商、各类技术外包服务商、电子商务咨询服务商、供应链优化及整合服务商及其他物流增值服务项目提供商（如供应链公司和跨境物流联盟）等在前人的研究中被称为寄生物种（张夏恒，2016；曹武军等，2019）。笔者认为"寄生"暗含"吸附"等义，为使表述更具客观性，从跨境电商生态系统中各物种与核心物种的关系紧密程度的角度，将这一群体称为"外围物种"。

以上四个物种构成了跨境电商的微观生态环境。

1.2.2.2 宏观环境因素

跨境电子商务的宏观环境包括政治因素（如政治制度、国家间的政治关系等）、经济因素（如各国的经济制度、经济发展水平等）、社会因素（如文化、宗教、人口组成、年龄阶段、道德标准、劳工保护等）、技术因素（互联网基础设施、移动网络和设备普及率等）、环境因素（如碳排放要求、卫生、安全标准等），以及法规因素（如进口国的关税、数量、品质、品类等要求和标准等）。跨境电子商务所面对的宏观环境是跨境电商长期稳定发展的基础和保证。当前不利的宏观环境体现在反全球化浪潮、世界经济下行、通货膨胀及中美贸易冲突等方面。

跨境电商的微观环境和宏观环境具有复杂性。互联网的全球化特征使得跨境电商能够直接满足不同国家消费者的需求，具有广阔的海外市场和商机。与此同时，商品在从卖方流向买方的过程中需要跨境进行，甚至经常需要跨越多国，因此，跨境交易常常同时涉及多个国家的通关和商检，涉及各地贸易中法务、税务、环保等方面的要求，涉及多种运输方式的选择与组合，增加了跨境电商物流产业链内外部环境的复杂性。

跨境电商的微观环境和宏观环境互相影响，各物种要素互相依赖。在跨境电子商务活动中，无论是跨境电商还是跨境物流、跨境支付等活动，都无法独立存在，生态系统中的各要素之间不断进行物质、信息或者能量的交换和互动。存在于跨境生态系统的各个要素都会受到各系统诸多要素的影响，构成子系统。在这个大量子系统相互协作的系统中，只有避免各个子系统之间相互消耗，维持各个子系统协同运行，才能达到整体增值的效应。现实中，各个子系统往往不能进行良好的配合，如容易受到信任机制、信息传输、交易成本等因素的干扰，导致价值链不能产生充分的效益，系统内部出现损耗。跨境物流供应链是跨境电商发展的关键环节，也有自己的生态系统。我们先从物流供应链的参与主体开始谈起。

1.3　跨境电商物流供应链的参与主体

跨境电商物流供应链是个链条式运行的整体，涵盖了采购、仓储、运输各个供应链管理环节的物流管理网络。作为跨境电商产业链上的重要支点，随跨境电商产业的逐渐发展，跨境电商物流供应链迎来了快速成长的新机遇。

从物理空间角度来说，跨境电商物流供应链流程分为输出国物流、国际物流、输入国物流，三者构成一个供应链，如图 1 - 5 所示。商品从卖家到买家的运输过程也是输出国物流 + 国际物流 + 输入国物流互相配合的过程，最终完成对消费者的服务。跨境物流供应链的最终目标围绕"降本增效 + 改善消费者体验"进行，是个不断精进、永无止境的过程。好的国际物流供应链意味着以更低的成本、更高的效率、更好的服务，完成消费者的良好购物体验。

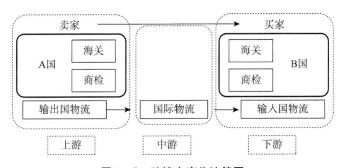

图 1 - 5　跨境电商物流简图

根据图 1 - 5，可以把跨境电商物流供应链分为上游、中游、下游三个部分。"上游"被称为"卖方"，可以是供应商和中间商，也可以是零售商及品牌商，他们是分布于综合性跨境电商平台、独立站平台及其他平台（如社交平台、短视频平台）上的第三方卖家。主流的跨境电商平台既有亚马逊、速卖通、Shopify、易贝、Wish、SheIn 等全球性平台，也有地区性平台，如 2016 年开始在东南亚布局的 Lazada、Shopee 等平台，还有各个国家的众多当地平台。在跨境电商平台上开设店铺的第三方卖家众多，构成庞大的卖方群体。

"中游"是各跨境物流供应链企业。运营模式按渠道类型主要分为国际商业快递、邮政大小包、跨境专线及海外仓、边境仓，以及保税区和自贸区物流等，既包括第三方物流公司，也包括整合第三方物流的物流集成商，即第四方物流公司和跨境物流联盟等形式。国际商业快递主要有美国的联合包裹服务公司（UPS）、TNT 与联邦快递（FedEx）和德国邮政（敦豪 DHL）等企业。邮政体系广泛、价格优惠，邮政大小包是国际快递 B2C 业务的主力。

"下游"被称为"买方"，包括商业买家（B2B）和个人买家（B2C、C2C），是整个跨境物流流程的最终用户，并来检验和评判整个物流流程的效果。物流服务的质量以消费者的体验为核心，也是跨境电商物流供应链不断发展的最终目标。三者的关系如图 1－6 所示。处于核心的跨境电商物流供应链连接着国内外的消费者。如对出口跨境物流来说，跨境电商平台和平台上的卖家是消费者，另一端的国外买家也是跨境物流的消费者，正是跨境物流把二者紧密联系起来，实现对双方的服务：以最低的成本、最高的效率，提供最好的服务。

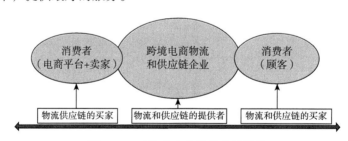

图 1－6 跨境电商物流供应链简图

1.4 跨境电商物流供应链生态系统

跨境物流一直是跨境电商的"痛点"，制约着跨境电商的顺畅发展。跨境物流供应链不仅涉及国内外海关和商检，也涉及国际物流运输，同样涉及微观环境和宏观环境的各个因素。以跨境电商生态系统为背景，跨境电商物流供应链也构成自己的生态系统，而这些影响跨境电商的因素共同构成了跨境物流供应链生态系统。

　　因为该生态系统影响因素繁多，其改进的困难程度也较大，很多学者对此展开了理论和实践研究，提出了自己的模型，试图改善跨境物流供应链生态圈的协同运行状况。跨境物流因此成为跨境电商的主流研究热点，以期达到"降本增效"、"提高服务"、"改善消费者体验"的目的。

1.4.1　文献回顾

　　曹武军等（2019）在图 1 - 3 的基础上，提出了物流企业主导型的跨境电商生态系统（图 1 - 7）。他们认为，物流企业主导型跨境电商生态系统是以物流企业及跨境电商平台为核心物种，结合支持物种、关键物种、寄生物种和内外环境因素，构成一个有机统一体。物流企业和跨境电商平台紧密结合，构成核心，维持跨境电商生态的运转，它强调了物流企业的重要性，把物流企业归为核心物种。

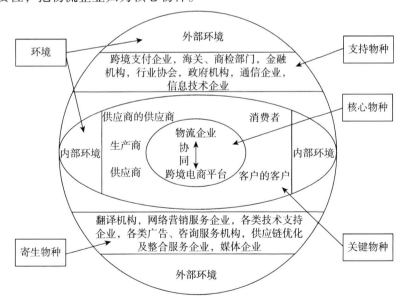

图 1 - 7　物流企业主导的融合型跨境电商生态系统

研究角度不同,构建的物流生态系统可能也会不同,谢泗薪、尹冰洁(2019)将跨境物流生态系统的构建置于中美贸易摩擦的背景中,提出跨境电商涉及政府、金融、商贸、通信等多方共同参与的综合物流体系。为解决物流供应链存在的难题,需要创新性地构建以基本运营、信息平台、产业集群等衔接融合为基础的智慧物流生态系统。

基于技术与跨境电商物流供应链的相生相伴属性,朱耿等(2018)将跨境电商和跨境物流生态系统相结合,利用人工智能技术诠释跨境物流供应链。以跨境电商物流运作为核心,以人工智能为支撑,构建跨境电商物流供应链生态系统。认为人工智能需以数字经济 + 平台经济 + 物流经济 + 贸易经济 + 金融经济为支柱,优质发展五大支柱经济的细分功能,逐步形成优质高效、深度融合的价值链、利益链、供应链和生态链,体现了链条思维和整合思维。

总之,物流生态系统是由物流企业生命有机体和与之相关的生存环境如信息技术和互联网技术等组成的复杂网络系统(薛晓芳、李雪,2017)。它将信息流、商流、物流、资金流有机结合并形成可持续协同循环的闭环系统,更侧重于整个链条的共同发展(张颖川,2015)。

1.4.2 跨境物流供应链生态系统再构建

在前人研究的基础上,本书重新构建跨境电商物流供应链生态系统,如图 1-8 所示。认为其是由支持物种、核心物种、关键物种、外围物种以及宏观环境共同构成。以出口为例,其核心物种为跨境电商物流供应链,依靠物流供应链平台连接其两端的消费者。跨境电商平台(包括平台上的卖家,卖家的生产供应商等)和境外的消费者,跨境支付企业等为支持物种。跨境营销、技术支持、广告和咨询等企业为外围物种,构成跨境物流供应链的微观环境。跨境电商物流供应链与跨境电商一样受同样的宏观外部环境制约,即由 PESTEL 因素构成的宏观环境。这也是本书的讨论框架,以此为基础,探讨跨境电商供应链要面对的挑战、风险、管理和优化。

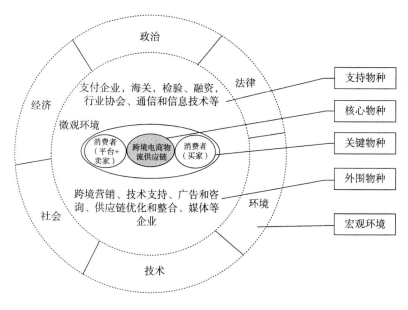

图 1-8　跨境物流供应链生态系统

1.5　跨境电商和物流供应链的协同

跨境电商与跨境物流供应链高度相关，二者彼此依赖，相辅相成，协同发展。跨境电商和跨境物流供应链作为跨境电商产业链中连接生产端和消费端的两个主体，二者在客户需求指向上一致。物流供应链的全部环节为跨境电商服务，跨境电商的市场扩展也会影响物流供应链的运营。

1.5.1　跨境电商对物流供应链有催化作用

随着电商的兴起，物流供应链承担起更严峻的任务。属于高科技业态的跨境电商如果与物流供应链活动融合，物流供应链的地位自然会提升。

跨境电商产生的强大物流供应链需求，促使物流活动明显增加。此外，跨境电商的不断发展，使物流供应链向网络化、智能化、一体化发展。要求物流企业在物流运输过程中降低成本，提高物流效率，改善消费者体验。

电商企业与物流企业的共同发展对于电商物流供应链的优化发展意义重大（Placzek，2010）。这种共同发展体现在，跨境电商的发展也使国际物流相关公司得以扩大客户来源和规模。物流活动也促使跨境电商产生的商品流量进行资源整合，散布在全国各地的经营商以及海外消费群体，通过物流系统的纽带形成贸易网络。

我国跨境电商发展势头强劲。2022 年 1—7 月，进出口总额达到 23.6 万亿元人民币，同比增长 10.4%。[①] 相应地，2022 年中国跨境电商进出口额 2.11 万亿元人民币，增长 9.8%。[②] 跨境电商对跨境物流业的拉动效应明显，二者基本保持同步增长，如图 1 - 9 所示（项姬秀，2021）。跨境电商的发展为物流供应链发展提供更好的市场机遇，其发展水平的高低也成为与物流链条融合的关键因素。物流企业需要产业结构优化升级来满足跨

图 1 - 9　跨境电商对跨境物流的拉动作用

---

① 数据概览：2022 年 1—7 月份外资外贸相关数据［EB/OL］．（2022 - 08 - 30）［2023 - 4 - 28］．https：//www.ndrc.gov.cn/fggz/fgzy/jjsjgl/202208/t20220830_1334678.html.

② 海关总署：2022 年我国跨境电商进出口 2.11 万亿元增长 9.8%［EB/OL］．（2023 - 01 - 13）［2023 - 4 - 28］．https：//m.gmw.cn/baijia/2023 - 01/13/36300544.html.

境电商发展的要求，在集群化、信息化和数字化等方面积极寻求提升，来实现跨境物流供应链整体水平的提升（项姬秀，2021）。

1.5.2　跨境物流对跨境电商有支撑作用

2023 年，全球疫情基本平稳，伴随全球经济的衰退，消费需求呈现疲软态势，跨境贸易受到一定的挑战。在这些因素的影响下，跨境电商需要更完善的物流供应链来提升消费者体验，才能穿越周期，实现长期良性发展。随着我国跨境电商规模不断增长，跨境物流供应链在跨境电商发展中的重要性与日俱增，对两者之间的关联度和匹配度要求更高，尤其要求跨境物流供应链的规模和效率继续提升。对于跨境物流对跨境电商的支撑作用，国内学者意见基本一致，因为大量的跨境电商交易最终都需要借助物流活动得以实现（苏杭，2017）。高集成化和数字化水平的国际物流模式可以支持跨境电商产业的发展。

跨境物流供应链目前已经成为跨境电商的核心竞争力。从物流本身而言，物流质量是跨境电商体验和质量的一个重要标志，物流的时效性、保质性等都是影响海外消费者评价跨境电商交易满意度的重要衡量指标（王宇楠，2022）。

从用户体验来看，跨境电商发展二十年来，跨境电商平台不断优化，交易规模逐渐增长，覆盖范围不断扩展。对消费者来说，前端平台美观便捷、产品质优价廉、交易方便快捷已不能满足其消费需求，消费者更加在意从下单到收到货物的时效，跨境物流的效率及服务质量成为影响跨境电商企业销售情况的重要因素（李航、黄昕怡，2021）。

若核心竞争力发展力度不足，无法推动跨境电商的发展，就会成为跨境电商发展的"痛点"。但跨境物流的降本增效，与其自身的复杂性息息相关，是一项长期而艰巨的任务。

1.6 跨境电商物流供应链的特点

不同于国内的物流供应链网络，跨境电商物流供应链更加复杂，环节流程更加繁复，因此面对的风险等级更高，各个环节的协同更具挑战性。

1.6.1 产业链条长而复杂

跨境电商物流距离远、时间长、成本高、流程复杂、可控性差，是跨境物流与国内物流的标志性差异。跨境物流中，头程运输可由海运、陆运、空运、专线等不同形式构成。薛磊等（2022）将跨境物流供应链的链条式结构分为七个环节，分别是前端揽收、仓储分拣、报关、干线运输、清关、海外仓储、尾程派送。七个环节又分为境内和境外两个大的模块，从揽收至报关可统称境内端，从清关至尾程派送可统称境外端。与传统国际贸易的物流环节相比，跨境电商物流在境内端增加了揽收分拣，在境外端增加尾程派送等环节，需要整体协调"最初一公里"的揽收环节和"最后一公里"的配送环节，因此，跨境物流供应链需要协调的环节更多，链条更加复杂。不同于传统的国际贸易，跨境电商的物流时效性要求高，这种时效性不仅仅是货物配送的时效性，也包括退换货的及时性。从这一点上来看，跨境物流对航空运输模式的需求较多，但航空运输价格高昂，这与跨境电商产品数量大、低客单价的特点相悖。这样的矛盾点制约着跨境电商物流效率的提升。这些矛盾点在跨境物流中集中体现为：第一，尾程配送效率差。在海外自建"最后一公里"配送环节的物流企业较少，需要跨境电商物流企业能够主动整合海外配送资源，实现本地化服务，打通全链条，改善消费体验，提供更好的服务。第二，退换货不及时。从客户主体来看，跨境电商物流的客户对象有很大一部分是个人客户，存在端到端、小批量、多批次以及高频率的退换货需求，客户通常以国内电商退换货的效率来要求跨境电商的退换货，这对于链条冗长的跨境物流供应链来说很难实现。

1.6.2　全链条资源整合的难度高

目前，跨境物流企业中能够有效贯穿上下游并提供端到端的第四方物流、物流集成商或物流联盟屈指可数。各国间政治制度、经济制度的不同，消费文化和消费习惯的差异，地缘政治的影响，后疫情时代的消费心理、区域经济体的建立等不利于全球经济一体化的因素深深影响跨境电商物流供应链的建立、维护和巩固。目前，我国跨境电商物流供应链仍呈现碎片化特征，服务区域较分散，物流企业的资源共享程度较低，发展不均衡，且资源整合度低，造成物流成本居高不下。全球各地的物流环境、海关报关要求、经济发展水平、各国文化等情况差异很大，使跨境物流比国内物流难度系数翻倍（慕艳平，2015）。

1.6.3　跨境物流供应链地区发展不平衡

我国跨境物流供应链主要集中在东南沿海地区，中西部地区较少，且规模较小，行业分散度高。珠三角、长三角、环渤海地区等经济发达，跨境运输需求旺盛，该地区航运、空运等基础设施相对完善，因此，交通资源的供应和竞争最为激烈。中西部地区经济相对不够活跃，跨境运输需求低，运输成本高，国际货运服务资源投入较少，其竞争表现为地域性和行业单一性。我国跨境物流竞争程度受财务实力、管理和技术能力的限制，以及我国物流市场相互分离等因素的影响，竞争特点表现为某区域、某行业或企业之间的竞争。如，长三角地区跨境物流公司之间的竞争；或者某单一行业之间资源的竞争，如3C行业①、电子产品制造业等，跨地区和跨

---

① 3C 是计算机（Computer）、通信（Communication）和消费电子产品（Consumer Electronics）三类电子产品的简称。

行业的竞争反而较少。随着跨境电商的需求增多，大多数跨境物流公司从单一的提供运输服务开始转向多元化服务，如与海外仓储公司之间进行合作，在跨境物流这一链条上，提供头程清关、仓储、配送，以及与亚马逊代发货服务（Fulfilment by Amazon，FBA）相关的诸多衍生和替代服务，如海外仓贴标换标、一件代发等。

第 2 章　跨境物流模式及提升理念

本章聚焦跨境电商物流供应链实践中的物流模式，分析物流模式中存在的风险和问题，探讨物流模式优化的理念、战略、业务操作和最后的目标。

跨境电商国际物流模式指的是跨境商品的流通采用何种渠道来完成。跨境电商国际物流供应链初期一般借助第三方物流完成，后来部分跨境电商平台也意识到物流供应链的重要性，初步搭建了自己的物流供应链系统，如速卖通国内段物流以菜鸟网络为基础，结合中国邮政国际快递及世界各国的邮政系统，进行全球配货。另外，菜鸟也建立了自己的物流专线。2023 年菜鸟与速卖通"全球 5 日达"国际快递快线产品上市，目标市场定位英国、荷兰、西班牙、比利时、韩国 5 国。国际快时尚电商巨头希音（SheIn）独立站针对快时尚的需求特点，建立了自己的物流供应链体系。国际巨头亚马逊已经建立了自己较为成熟的 FBA 物流配送系统，以海外仓实现高效的物流供应链管理。一个共同的规律是，物流供应链的构建和维护成本十分高昂，投资成本回收周期长。如亚马逊已经建立了自己较为成熟的 FBA 仓储体系，但成本高昂，需要投入大量资金，利润周期长，使得 FBA 物流仓储的费用不断攀升[①]，给卖家带来了不少压力。总体来说，

---

① FBA 费用增加 5%，利润或消失 20%，卖家要扛不住了［EB/OL］.（2022 - 04 - 28）［2023 - 04 - 28］. https：//www. sohu. com/a/542139104_115514.

中国跨境物流以中国邮政＋第三方物流为主，第四方物流不断出现，以及物流集成商和跨境物流联盟的构思，都是未来跨境物流供应链的发展方向。

2.1 跨境电商国际物流模式

目前跨境电商国际物流的主要模式包括国际邮政大小包、国际商业快递、海外仓、国际物流专线、边境仓、保税区与自贸区物流等。各模式互相配合，发挥物流供应链的功能。

2.1.1 中国邮政大小包

中国邮政大小包是中国跨国物流的主要方式，它借助万国邮政体系实现商品的进出口输运。据不完全统计，我国目前跨境电子商务有超过70%的商品是通过邮政体系进行运输的，其中中国邮政占据50%左右的份额。[①]在国际邮政小包中，使用较多的有中国邮政、香港邮政、比利时邮政、俄罗斯邮政和德国邮政等。邮政网络覆盖面广，价格低廉，清关方便，但运输时间长，普通包裹丢包率高，非挂号件无法跟踪，且在商品体积、重量、形状等方面局限性较大，适合运输价值不高的零售商品。

2.1.2 国际商业快递

国际商业快递主要指 UPS、FedEx、DHL、TNT 四大商业快递巨头。国际商业快递优点明显，运输和配送能力强、速度快、客户体验好，但价格

① 跨境电商物流的主要模式有哪些？［EB/OL］.（2020 - 12 - 17）［2023 - 04 - 28］. https：//www.cifnews.com/article/85581?ivk_sa = 1024320u.

高昂（曹武军等，2019）。如使用 UPS 从中国寄包裹到美国，最快可在 48 小时内到达。此外，我国本土快递公司也逐步涉入跨境物流供应链业务，如顺丰供应链①、申通等。国际商业快递可以针对不同的顾客群体，如按国家地域、商品种类、体积大小、商品重量等的不同，选取不同的渠道实现商品的速递。总之，国际商业快递具有时效性高、丢包率低等优点，但价格高，尤其在偏远地区的附加费更高，有时含电等特殊类商品无法速递。

2.1.3 海外仓

海外仓是跨境物流供应链的热点，也是中国政策的支持点。海外仓要求在跨境电商消费国租赁或建设仓库，先通过头程运输把商品送达海外仓库备货，然后通过跨境电商平台销售商品，接到顾客订单后从海外仓库直接发货与配送。海外仓可以由跨境电商平台建设或租赁，更多由第三方物流企业自建或租赁，平台和第三方物流企业进行合作。如，美国的亚马逊、易贝等跨境电子商务推出官方合作的海外仓，中国的第三方物流企业顺丰等物流公司也逐步涉足海外仓业务。

海外仓被认为是跨境物流供应链的创新和突破，有望弥补国际邮政大小包和国际商业快递的短板，如物流时效、物流成本、海关与商检、本土化、退换货等问题。但海外仓的租赁、建设与运营前期需要投入巨大的成本，利润周期长（如亚马逊的周期可能是在 10 年，这对投资资本来说是个挑战②）。海外仓的选址、大小等都是需要考虑的问题，需要单独的法人公司运营，也需要专业的人员与资金，且在商品预运前要有准确的销售预期，否则，商品在头程运输后会因滞销而造成库存与积压，造成仓储成本上升，挤压利润。

---

① 收购 DHL 在华供应链业务后，顺丰供应链加速数智化布局［EB/OL］. 第一财经，（2021 – 07 – 09）［2023 – 04 – 28］. https：//baijiahao. baidu. com/s?id = 1704786789979882738&wfr = spider&for = pc.

② Amazon Empire：The Rise and Reign of Jeff Bezos［EB/OL］.［2023 – 1 – 20］. https：//www. bilibili. com/video/av93595636/.

2.1.4 国际物流专线

货物的运输量达到一定稳定的规模后，国际物流专线是个不错的选择。国际物流专线是针对某一特定国家或地区的跨境专线递送方式，它的物流起点、物流终点、运输工具、运输线路、运输时间都基本固定。物流时效较国际邮政小包快，物流成本较国际快递低，且保证清关。对固定路线的跨境电子商务而言，不失为一种较好的物流解决方案。但国际物流专线具有区域和数量的局限性，是其突出的弊端。国际物流专线主要包括航空专线、港口专线、铁路专线、大陆桥专线以及固定多式联运专线，如中欧班列各条线路，到俄罗斯的燕文物流，顺丰深圳—台北全货机航线[①]等都是运行不错的线路。

2.1.5 边境仓

边境仓是指在跨境电子商务目的国的邻国边境内租赁或建设仓库，通过物流将商品预先运达仓库，通过跨境电商平台接收顾客订单后，从边境仓库发货。根据所处地域的不同，边境仓可分为绝对边境仓和相对边境仓。绝对边境仓指跨境电子商务的交易双方所在国家相邻，将仓库设在卖方所在国家，且与买方所在国家相邻近的城市，如我国对俄罗斯的跨境电子商务交易，在哈尔滨或中俄边境的中方城市设立仓库。相对边境仓指跨境电子商务的交易双方不相邻，将仓库设在买方所在国家的相邻国家的边境城市，如我国对巴西的跨境电子商务交易，在与之相邻的阿根廷、巴拉圭、秘鲁等接壤国家的临近边境城市设立仓库。相对边境仓对买方所在国而言属于边境仓，对卖方所在国而言属于海外仓。海外仓的运营需要成本，商品存在积压风险，送达后的商品很难再退回国内，这些因素推动着

---

① "巨无霸"全货机加盟深圳—台北航线 [EB/OL]. (2015 - 3 - 23) [2023 - 1 - 20]. http://www.taihainet.com/news/twnews/bilateral/2015 - 03 - 23/1383416.html.

绝对边境仓的发展，如对俄罗斯跨境电子商务中，我国在哈尔滨设立的边境仓。另外，一些国家的税收政策和政局不稳定、货币贬值、严重的通货膨胀，这些因素也会刺激边境仓的出现。如巴西税收政策十分严格，海外仓成本很高，在其接壤国家的边境设立边境仓，利用南方共同市场（自由贸易协定），推动对巴西的跨境电子商务就是一种降低成本、提高效率的方法。

2.1.6　保税区、自贸区物流

由于中国独特的产业优势、贸易环境和政策，我国的进口业务较多使用保税区或自由贸易区（以下简称"自贸区"）物流。它是先将商品运送到保税区或自贸区仓库，通过跨境电商平台获得顾客订单后，通过保税区或自贸区仓库进行分拣、打包等，集中运输，并进行物流配送。这种方式具有集货物流和规模化物流的特点，有利于缩短物流时间，降低物流成本。如亚马逊以中国（上海）自由贸易试验区为入口，引入全球商品线，跨境电子商务企业可以先把商品放在自贸区，当顾客下单后，将商品从自贸区发出，有效缩短配送时间。通过自贸区或保税区仓储，可以有效利用自贸区与保税区的各类政策、综合优势与优惠措施，尤其利用各保税区和自贸区在物流、通关、商检、收付汇、退税方面的便利，简化跨境电子商务的业务操作，实现促进跨境电子商务交易的目的。

2.2　跨境物流供应链的参与主体

目前，跨境电商物流供应链一般由第三方物流公司或第四方物流公司为主体作为任务的发起者来完成商流的转移。具体来讲，跨境物流供应链的实际运行主要由第三方物流公司完成。买方、卖方以外的第三方物流专业企业，以服务外包、合同委托的模式承担企业的物流服务。国内电商自建物流相对容易，但跨境电子商务物流供应链复杂，物流投入要求高。虽然个别跨境电商平台试图搭建自建物流体系，但基于资金、跨境物流的复杂性和各种宏观因素障碍，大多数跨境电商选择第三方物流模式，如与邮政、国际快递公司合作等。即便是邮政或者国际快递公司，在一些国家与地区，也会选择与当地的第三方物流公司合作，进行最后的尾程配送。跨境物流链条由多种模式、多个第三方物流企业通力合作，完成物流服务。或者由第四方物流公司搭建平台，第三方物流公司作为功能性服务提供者，完成货物配送。包括我国在内的大批海洋运输企业、国际货代企业，拥有丰富的进出口贸易、海外运作经验和海外业务网点布局及国际化操作能力，它们都是跨境电商和跨境物流供应链的合作对象。

第四方物流公司指专为交易双方、第三方物流提供物流规划、咨询、物流信息系统、供应链管理等活动的组织，它通过调配与管理自身及具有互补性的服务提供商的资源、能力和技术，提供综合、全面的供应链解决方案（赵广华，2014）。第四方物流的优势在于其资源整合能力：通过整个供应链的影响力，在解决企业物流的基础上，整合各类社会资源，实现物流信息共享与对社会物流资源的充分利用。优秀的第四方物流可以整合全球各地物流配送服务资源，能够提供开放比价竞价、全球智能路径优化、多物流商协同配送、自动打单跟单、大数据智能分析等服务。虽然跨境电子商务与跨境物流具有较高的复杂性，但我国第四方物流公司开始出现，成为跨境物流的新生力量。

无论是第三方物流公司还是第四方物流公司，进口时都可以使用直邮、包税进口等方式。在出口时，为达到节约成本的目的，一般使用集货物流，先将商品运输到本地或当地的仓储中心，达到一定数量或形成一定规模后，通过与国际物流公司合作，将商品运到境外买家手中；或者将中国各地发来的商品先行聚集，再批量配送到世界各地；或者一些商品品类类似的跨境电子商务企业建立战略联盟，成立共同的跨境物流运营中心，利用规模优势或优势互补的理念，达到降低跨境物流费用的目的。如米兰网在广州与成都自建了仓储中心，商品在仓储中心聚集后，通过与国际快递合作将商品发至国外买家。

2.3 跨境物流供应链模式的问题

2.3.1 物流模式初级，地区差异大

目前，各物流模式中的功能性物流公司大都规模较小，以中小物流供应链公司居多，其业务面窄，国内物流地区发展不平衡，国外物流地区差异大。随着国际贸易和跨境电商的发展，中国的物流公司逐渐增多，主要集中在长三角、珠三角以及环渤海沿岸等经济发达地区。内陆和西部地区的跨境物流系统和公司数目与沿海地区存在较大差距。中国物流的业务面与国际商业快递相比，存在较大差距。中国前十大国际物流公司的业务量总和与国际四大快递公司相比，仍然有较大差距。中国远洋物流、中铁快运、中邮物流、德邦物流、中储发展股份有限公司、南方物流集团等有国资背景者较多，与国外的商业快递在运营模式和效率方面存在较大差距，在信息系统、价值理念等方面尚有很大的提升空间。无论是进口物流还是出口物流，各个平台的物流服务公司不同，运输和配送效率不同。物流供应链的稳定性、灵活性、快速反应能力等受政治环境、经济环境、运输线路、社会事件（如罢工、冲突）等影响较大，售后服务缓慢，购物体验仍有很大的发展空间。对欧美等业务量大的地区的物流运输和配送时间与业务量不大、经济不发达的地区的物流运输和配送时间差异较大。主要瓶颈仍然是成本高，效率低，服务和体验有待提升。

2.3.2 物流模式分散，网络链接不紧密

上文提到的我国跨境电商各种国际物流模式在各自的领域内发挥着运输配送的功能，但业务量与国外大物流企业的业务量（如运送包裹量）相

比较小，运力水平有限，运输和自动分拣等自动化水平较低且分散。如物流公司设计自己的物流供应链系统，覆盖尽量多的地区和国家，资金和资源平摊后，造成资源的浪费，网络系统的整体水平低且重复发展现象严重。物流和物流公司之间、各物流模式之间的信息流不能畅通、共享，成本高但效率低。

目前的物流模式混用、共用现象多。一方面是环节多、流程复杂；另一方面是物流水平参差不齐，很难用单一物流模式贯穿始终，各模式混用后效率低，整合能力仍有待增强。未来的物流供应链应加强其整合能力，发展差异化服务，而不是多种模式共存，这样不利于效率的提高。另外，在与本地公司的对接中，也存在网链不畅、信息系统不能共享等由利益冲突导致的成本上升。

2.3.3　思维模式初级，价值链思维有待增强

以价值链思维整合物流供应链是长远的发展目标。如在物流外包模式中，借助第三方本地物流进行"最后一公里"的配送，服务质量参差不齐。需要第四方物流公司在当地进行物流资源整合，提高服务水平，统一服务质量，促进电商经济的发展和物流产业的发展，整合数据和基础平台，提供差异化、集约化的供应链解决方案，实现物流、商流、资金流、信息流和商检与清关的配合，提升链条的增值能力。

2.4　跨境物流供应链模式的提升

既然跨境物流成为影响未来跨境电子商务发展的制约因素，物流供应链模式的改善会有利于跨境电商的发展。国际物流供应链的优化，对构建跨境电商的核心竞争力尤为重要。基于生态系统的视角和当前跨境电商发展的实际环境，本节将尝试对跨境电商物流供应链模式的提升从理念、战

略、业务实操和最终目标四个维度分别阐述。

2.4.1 理念的提升：整合性思维

我国跨境电商物流的历史不长，处在发展的初期阶段，需要以整合性思维为理念，不断地进行优化组合，才能实现更好的发展。

2.4.1.1 现实和理论依据

相比于跨境电商，国内电商发展成熟，生态系统良好，资金流、物流、信息流和商流顺畅，成为世界最大的电子商务市场。相比国内电商的良好发展，我国跨境电商整体表现较分散、弱小，虽然经营主体达到70.5万户、从业人员达到301.4万人，但经营规模超过1000万元以上的企业占比小于10%，总体上仍处在发展初期（祁飞，2020）。国外跨境电商起步早，发展时间长，更好地利用了电子商务的红利期，积累了更多的经验，占领了更多的先机，国际支付手段更加便捷，如 PayPal 在全球有着更强的跨境支付能力，亚马逊等平台经过十几年的经验积累和持续投资，在世界各地尤其在发达国家的电子商务市场已经占据了更加有利的地位。世界较大的电商市场如美国和欧洲国家，它们在制度距离、文化距离、消费习惯、经济发展水平等方面更加接近，更加有利于开拓本地市场，已经有了先发制人的优势。

西方电商如亚马逊等有更好的物流配送能力。四大国际商业快递企业起步早、资金投入多、理念超前，发展强劲，是国际商业物流的主力。相比之下，我国跨境电商物流服务资源分散，市场集中度低。邮政小包是目前的主流国际物流配送模式，为提高国际物流配送能力，必须使用四大国际商业快递等物流渠道才能完成供应链的运作，完成高效配送。但国际商业快递的高成本和中国商品的匹配度不总是统一的。商业快递更适合价值高、体积小的高档物品，对跨境客单价不高的零售商品的成本构成较大的压力，不利于成本核算。尽管邮政和商业快递这两种主流的物流模式盛行，但这两种模式局限于速度慢、运输量小且成本高，不利于提升中国国际物流的竞争力，不利于物流供应链的发展。目前国内物流供应链的发展重任主要由跨国公司承担，集中在某些特定的行业，如铁路、粮食、家电、电子、汽车产业链等（杜志平，2020）。我国跨境电商物流产业链的发展仍然处在初级阶段。

根据生命周期理论，企业和产业的发展要经过萌芽、发展、成长、成熟、衰退等阶段。生命周期的不同阶段匹配不同的组织管理模式和经营模式。作为跨境电商发展的重要支撑和关键环节，跨境国际物流供应链受跨境电商生命周期的制约，也受物流供应链生命周期的制约。因此，物流企业首先要考虑自身所处生命周期的阶段以确定跨境物流发展模式。2017年至2022年，我国跨境电商交易规模5年增长了近10倍，跨境电商产业进入快速发展期，但仍处在发展初期。跨境电商物流供应链产业资源分散、市场集中度低，资源利用率低，也处在发展初期。国家发展改革委统计数据表明，2021年，我国社会物流总费用与GDP的比率为14.6%，较2012年下降了3.4个百分点，尽管与主要经济体差距不断缩小，但仍然存在不小的差距，而且短时间内很难补上。因此，《"十四五"现代物流发展规划》将"推动物流提质增效降本"作为"十四五"时期现代物流发展的重要任务，明确提出到2025年，社会物流总费用与GDP的比率较2020年下降2个百分点左右。为了物流供应链的更好发展，需要依托良好的宏观环境，加大整合能力。这是物流产业发展的挑战，更是物流产业发展的机遇，跨境物流也面临同样的挑战和机遇。

实践中，整合是企业和产业发展的内在要求。企业要面对不断变化的市场和客户需求，宏观环境和微观环境都在不断变化当中，企业的管理在内外环境的夹击中主动求变、进行整合也是企业不断发展的内在要求。消费者会选择更好的消费体验、高效的售后服务、利于环境的包装和更加低廉的价格，因此企业的产品要不断地更新，满足、创造不同的需求变化。企业内部的要素整合可以释放更大的成本和效率空间，提供更好的物流方案。产业的发展受制于外部环境。宏观大环境的变化有时难以控制，如自然灾害、疫情、政治冲突、贸易摩擦、地缘政治、区域经济一体化、反全球化浪潮等会给产业的发展带来弊端和不利影响。不断变化的不利因素迫使企业和产业进行结构调整、战略调整，用更新的理念应对内外环境的变化，因此要有整合性思维。

2.4.1.2　整合性思维

整合性思维也即集成思维、一体化思维（祁飞，2020），是网链思维、协同思维（张夏恒、郭海玲，2016；张夏恒，2016；付帅帅等，2021；米岩，2022）、融合思维（王宇楠，2022）在物流供应链中的体现。物流供应链的整合意味着既要整合资源，又要整合物流供应链模式，从供应链、价值链协调发展的角度整合跨境电商系统内有利于物流、供应链的一切资源。不但要从宏观上进行整合，努力创造有利的环境，更多地要从微观上进行整合，包括政策的整合、区域的整合、物流企业间的整合、物流企业内部的整合等。要利用一体化整合思维，从更大的角度、更宽的场景、更远大的目标出发，做出长期的发展规划。具体来说，从跨境电商国际物流供应链模式整合的物流一体化方向看，国际物流模式优化更需要关注商品与物流模式的匹配度：以供应链管理思想为核心，制订一体化物流解决方案，构建跨境电商核心竞争力。

2.4.2　战略的提升：一体化物流供应链解决方案

针对跨境电商国际物流模式的整合，一体化物流供应链解决方案是最佳战略。跨境电商的竞争也是物流供应链的竞争，因此对供应链各环节进行整合优化，设计高效的物流解决方案，能够实现效益的最大化，促进跨境电商的发展。对跨境电商来说，跨境电商供应链包括制造商、供应商、国际物流公司、仓储中心、分销商及国外顾客，这些要素构成了一个网络，管理的载体是贯穿于"链"条中的商品流、物流、资金流和信息流。物流是跨境电商供应链中的"桥梁"，服务于整条跨境电商供应链。对此，新时代下物流企业必须深入"端到端"的供应链运营中，创新供应链服务，形成新型经营模式，发挥物流在整条供应链中的支撑作用。

跨境电商国际物流作业环节包括接单、收货、仓储、分拣、转运、包装、装卸以及商检、国际结算、清关、售后服务等，这些流程构成了整体供应链的物流子系统，涉及不同国家与不同的国际物流企业。鉴于此，应加强跨境电商国际供应链各物流节点的协同意识，物流模式的选择应整合供应链各环节的关系，强化各环节之间的关联性、协同性和相互支持性。

2.4.3 业务实操的提升：微观和宏观

跨境电商物流供应链的具体业务实践和操作可以从微观和宏观两个方面的业务展开。

2.4.3.1 微观业务

首先，物流业务和流程的系统化和一体化整合。仓储、配送、包装、转运、装卸、售后服务、退换货、商检、国际结算、清关等环节要系统化，尤其是跨境运输、清关等节点问题是物流企业必须顺利解决的问题，这样才能制定出最优物流解决方案。不管是第三方物流企业还是第四方物流企业，针对市场情况，培养企业的核心竞争力都将是一个长期的可持续性任务。

其次，物流供应链的信息化。要以信息化为主导，整合跨境电商国际物流服务平台。信息化是跨境电商国际物流整合的重要依托，统一的信息平台构建是实现跨境电商物流互联互通的有效路径。要针对跨境电商物流中心需求的变化，整合集成接单、收货、仓储、转运、包装、装卸以及商检、国际结算、清关等物流环节，需要构建跨境电商物流统一信息平台，以满足物流企业各职能部门的信息采集需求。整合也要包括物流企业的内部库存管理、信息系统、配送系统等一体化整合。跨境物流的信息追踪要做到全程化信息透明、可追踪、准确。信息的整合是物流一体化的基础，建立在信任机制之上的信息化既深度触达厂商、仓库，又深度连接消费者，是跨境物流一体化的保证。

再次，细化物流模式的组合和匹配度。对产品的特征、时效、成本等不同条件进行综合考量，选取最优物流模式组合，短期内仍将是最优选择。在选择物流渠道商时要考虑的因素不仅要基于物流企业经验层面、服务层面及实力层面，还要与外在宏观因素精准匹配，以便选取低成本、高效率的国际物流模式。差异化服务将是更加明智的选择，把物流成本和效率通过市场渠道进行表现，为消费者提供可选择的差异化物流服务将更加符合当前的实际情况。

最后，本地化服务和海外仓。为提供更好的体验，本地化服务是跨境物流发展的最终归宿。海外仓是本地化服务的具体表现。因此，我国政府大力发展海外仓，鼓励第三方物流企业自建或租用海外仓。海外仓可以降低运输成本，加快发货速度，而且能做到销售、配送本土化，提高消费者购物体验，所以海外仓将是跨境电商国际物流模式的主流（庞燕，2015；冀芳、张夏恒，2015；祁飞，2020）。不过，海外建仓需要大量的资金投入，需要良好的跨境电商业务的支持和良好的全球化经济背景。在全球经济不景气的大背景下，电商经济 2022 年末整体下滑，电商平台业务萎缩、裁员，美元波动，面临的风险增多，资本投入谨慎，海外仓的风险承受能力下降，慎重建仓、缩减海外仓的情况偶有出现。而且，海外仓更适合有实力的跨境电商和第三方物流企业，而中小跨境电商卖家依托物流公司，形成紧密联盟，能够取得更大的集成效果。总之，经济大环境是海外仓发展的基础，只有国际经济出现良好的发展势头，海外仓才能得到更大的发展，才能促进跨境电商的发展。

2.4.3.2 宏观操作

首先，整合思维下的物流一体化意味着物流企业能提供物流一体化能力的解决方案，即企业更具备物流资源的外部整合能力，也是企业整合上游、中游、下游全供应链资源的能力。具体可以表现在物流集成商、第四方物流或跨境物流联盟的建立方面。无论是物流集成商还是以第四方物流为核心的物流联盟，都讲究整个供应链的资源整合、资源利用的效率，强调各参与方的协同发展（冀芳、张夏恒，2015；米岩，2022），形成物流供应链内部生态系统的共生和发展。一是把生产、物流、销售和消费者的供应链进行一体化和系统化，也就是把生产者、跨境电商平台和消费者连接起来；二是把物流、资金流、信息流统一起来，形成信任团体。

其次，以供应链管理为核心定制一体化物流解决方案。在信息化、全球化推动下，产业链升级进一步促进供应链向一体化服务转变。国际物流企业需要系统梳理供应链各节点上物流需求的变化，通过流程再造和物流资源整合，形成供应链一体化的新型物流服务体系。建设基于价值链理论的国际物流网络协同体系，一体化的物流解决方案是要加强国际物流网络协同及各物流节点间协同，鼓励具有海外仓储运营经验的物流公司建立独立的海外仓。

再次，营造良好的国际环境。全球化是跨境电商发展的最佳环境。在反全球化的各因素作用下，跨境物流供应链生态系统的 6 大宏观因素在当今状态下尤为重要。如果说科技和信息系统等微观因素是跨境电商发展所需的"水分"，宏观环境则是跨境电商发展的"空气"。2022 年末，跨境电商平台的成交金额数据再次表明，宏观环境因素的改变会给跨境电商的发展带来巨大影响，如知识产权的保护、社会文化的距离等将对跨境电商长期的发展产生至关重要的影响。未来更应该为创造一个健康、开放、包容的国际良好环境而努力，对政治、经济、社会、技术环境、法律等因素逐一进行改善，是跨境电商物流供应链发展的基础保证。

最后，人才的培养。人才是物流供应链整合的保证。我国国际物流起步晚，发展处于初级阶段，现在还缺乏完全适合国际物流企业发展的人才。跨境物流人才的素质要求较高，既要有宏观视野，又要有对业务细节的把握，目前高校等培养的人才不能满足物流供应链产业的要求。拥有国际经验，熟悉国际规则，实现跨文化发展，多种能力综合发展的专业性人才的锻炼和培养将是物流产业发展的保证。政府、企业和高校等机构应提高认识，紧密配合，培养跨境物流专业人才。

2.4.4 提升目标：降本增效、优化服务

"降本增效、优化服务"一直是物流供应链追求的目标。在这一目标

的指引下，对企业来说，降低物流成本，提高物流运输和配送效率，提供更加优质的服务，是跨境电商物流供应链企业的努力方向。对消费者来说，能便捷地买到质优价廉的商品，有良好的购物体验，也是内在需求。二者是一个问题的两个方面。为提供优质的服务，物流企业要努力提高物流供应链的响应能力，提高应对风险的能力，保证服务的连续性和高效性（杜志平，2020；庞燕，2015），这是跨境电商的核心竞争力之一，也是验证国际物流供应链价值的最终标准（祁飞，2020）。

第3章　跨境电商物流供应链的
困境和风险评估

本章基于物流供应链生态系统，从跨境电商物流供应链生态系统出发，从宏观和微观两个角度，分析其存在的各种困境、风险。本章内容也构成本书第4章优化方案的基础。

3.1　我国跨境电商物流供应链的困境

在跨境电商的发展中，商流和物流的发展落后于信息流和资金流的发展，成为跨境电商发展的制约因素。我国物流供应链起步较晚，基础设施、管理理念、管理水平都比较落后，面临多方面的困境（赵广华，2014）。

3.1.1　成本居高不下

成本是跨境物流供应链高度关注的问题之一。相较国内快递，跨境电商物流的距离远，物流费率高。相比传统外贸物流，跨境电商物流需求碎片化、运输频次高，同时全链路物流环节更多，也导致物流费率升高。影响跨境电商物流成本的因素中，跨境物流运输（头程运输）是主要因素。在跨境物流运输中，包装费、人工费、管理费、仓位费等，都是大成本消耗，会挤压跨境电商平台及卖家的利润空间。专线物流成本尽管比商业快递低，但灵活性较差，由于很难精准预测与把控国外市场，会出现货品积压，从而增加存货成本。再加上该物流方案中"最后一公里"配送的覆盖面较少，会增加物流配送成本。跨境电商所售小件商品通常通过国际商业快递和国际邮政小包运送，如国际 E 邮宝、DHL、FedEx、UPS、TNT 等，虽然能够保证时效，但运费居高不下（杨子等，2018；赵广华，2014）。运费的增加必然导致商品成本增加，这样就大大削弱了中国商品的价格优势，从而降低了中国商品的国际竞争力。

3.1.2　供应链效率低

跨境物流供应链的效率主要体现在以下两个方面。一是通关效率不高。有些国家的跨境商检、清关等手续的程序复杂，基础设施落后；存在商品的手续不够齐全、数量少报、质量不过关等问题。此外，对于目的国的相关商品包装质量等法律法规了解不足，导致产品包装不合格，产品说明不清晰，商标侵犯知识产权等问题，严重影响通关效率。二是运输和配送效率有待提升。长距离的跨境运输，尤其是海上运输的时间成本巨大，导致物品到达消费者手中的时间较长。跨境电商物流配送的速度是影响境外买家购买的重要因素。欧美等地客户对时效性的要求较高，如配送时间超出预期，往往会接到投诉，甚至造成交易失败。根据相关数据，中国邮政小包送至亚洲邻国需 5～10 天；送至欧美主要国家需 7～15 天；送至其他国家和地区需 15～30 天（赵广华，2014）。长配送周期很容易导致货物严重积压，配送时间更长，恶性循环加剧。例如，小额交易卖家最常选用的香港邮政小包曾多次因业务量过多导致货物囤积，效率难以保证。此外，由于运输距离长，从物流员工揽件到最后将物品送交到用户的手上需要经历多次转运，难免会出现包裹破损的情况，甚至会出现丢件现象。这些都是跨境供应链效率低的表现。

3.1.3　集成化水平低

我国第三方物流企业虽然数量较多，但整体发展尚处于从成长期向成熟期过渡的阶段，结构多样、规模较小，并呈粗放型发展态势。大型且专业化程度较高的第三方物流企业较少。大多数物流企业提供的是国内物流服务，对于国际快递服务，主要以普通快递或邮政大小包等形式进行，能够提供国内物流、国际物流和目的国物流集成化服务的物流公司较少。目前为跨境电商提供国际快递服务的仍然主要是国际四大商业快递公司。尽管中国邮政速递物流公司（Express Mail Service，EMS）、顺丰速运公司等后来居上，但仍需积累跨境物流资本和经验。

3.1.4　数字化水平低

虽然跨境物流信息化和数字化水平已经得到大幅提升，但在实际运行中，跨境电子商务企业的组织结构和管理模式通常较简单，在库存管理方面缺乏数字化思维，库存的预测与实际销售往往产生差异，导致库存成本控制不科学。尤其是海外仓的运营，精准的销售预测是海外仓精准控制仓储的关键，数字化水平的高低直接影响着海外仓运营的成本和效率。数字化水平低也导致部分跨境物流交易存在物流信息不详细、追踪不及时。同时，受限于不同国家的信息化发展水平和信息技术标准不同，物流企业之间的物流信息系统很难做到有效衔接，导致物流信息滞后，消费者很难及时追踪到商品所处的运输环节、所在的地点，从而大大影响跨境购物体验。总而言之，跨境电商物流供应链只有以信息技术为基础才能发展，而缺乏数字管理思想会导致多种问题，如静态库存管理落后、供应链管理能力低、无法对消费者需求和市场变化做出快速准确的响应等，无法满足消费者对物流服务的追踪需求等问题（蒲新蓉，2022）。数字化发展水平低，不能与公司发展速度相匹配，将导致跨境物流企业抗经营风险能力弱，物流供应链韧性下降，无法对抗因跨境电商发展而产生的各类经营风险。

3.1.5　海外仓资源整合程度低

海外仓是跨境电商重要的境外节点，是新型物流基础设施。海外仓真正的价值在于全方位整合，在物流方面主要体现在供应链的整合，从而降低物流成本。例如，随着跨境电商的商品品类逐渐增多和升级，以家居、户外产品为代表的大货、重货越来越多，而跨境电商的参与者以中小企业为主，难以通过高成本的配送方式来配送大件货物，海外仓成为必然选择。主流电商平台如易贝（eBay）、亚马逊等鼓励，甚至要求中国卖家更多地采用海外仓方式发货，以保证用户体验。有些物流公司尝试选择成熟的市场建设海外仓，如俄速递（Ruston）在俄罗斯联合建立"海外仓"，广州的"出口易"也在英、美、澳、俄罗斯和西班牙等地自建仓储中心。但海外仓的建设及运营成本较高，主要适用于货价较高、对物流成本承担能力较强，且市场销量较大的商品。海外仓由资金实力雄厚的卖家封闭运营，与中小电商企业小额产品的资源共享度较低。因此，大多数成熟的海外仓不对中小企业开放，很难实现有限的海外仓资源的共享。以上问题主要体现在微观层面；宏观来讲主要体现在以下 2 个方面。

3.1.6　全球经济衰退的预期

物流供应链的投资巨大，需要发展稳定的跨境电商产业的支撑。2020年以来，全球经济衰退，风投资本对跨境电商物流供应链的投资较为谨慎。跨境电商物流产业链利润较薄，需要长期经营回收成本，不稳定的全球经济环境更增加了投资的风险，预期收益低。此外，全球合作的趋势被区域经济一体化条块分割，区域全面经济伙伴关系协定（Regional Comprehensive Economic Partnership，RCEP）、全面与进步跨太平洋伙伴关系协定（Comprehensive and Progressive Agreement for Trans-Pacific Partnership，CPTPP）、美墨加三国协议（The United States-Mexico-Canada Agreement，USMCA）的运行阻碍了世界经济贸易组织等国际组织的作用，反全球化浪潮不利于经济一体化的发展，更不利于跨境电商物流供应链的建立和维护。此外，跨境电商平台亚马逊、易贝、速卖通等近期裁员的消息有可能使跨境电商产业进入调整阶段，跨境物流产业链也会做相应的调整。

3.1.7 系统的不稳定因素增多

作为复杂的跨境电商物流供应链生态系统，每个物种都存在一定的风险和挑战，内部企业、产业的微观环境与国家间宏观环境的协调总会出现不一致的情况。另外，信任机制的建立、知识产权的保护、数据传输和隐私的保护、区块链等先进技术的广泛应用仍然需要时间的检验和企业的不断尝试。各国之间仍需要不断的沟通，在探讨建立新的规则、标准和模式中慢慢推进跨境电商和物流产业的发展。

3.2 跨境电商物流供应链风险评估

在跨境电子商务环境下，跨境物流服务涉及较多的风险因素，例如，多种物流模式、海关清关、第三方支付平台以及互联网信息等，这些因素又会因为多个国家的政治、法律、经济以及所处的地理环境等而具有多样化的特点，其存在的风险隐患程度也具有很大的差异性（高帆，2020）。不少学者对风险的识别和评估进行了研究，大致分为内部风险和外部风险两类，与跨境电商物流供应链生态系统的微观环境和宏观环境一致。

3.2.1 第三方跨境物流供应链风险研究

跨境电商在选择第三方跨境物流时要做风险识别，居永梅（2020）将其风险分为内部风险和外部风险（图 3 - 1），细分成 8 个维度，涵盖 28 个风险因子。内部风险主要涵盖战略风险、合作风险、供应风险以及信息风险，均为跨境电商内部以及合作中面临的风险；外部风险主要包括运输风险、包装仓储风险、环境风险、装卸风险以及海关风险，主要涉及第三方物流企业。对其风险因子进行权重分析后，认为合作风险是跨境电商选择第三方物流时面临的主要风险。

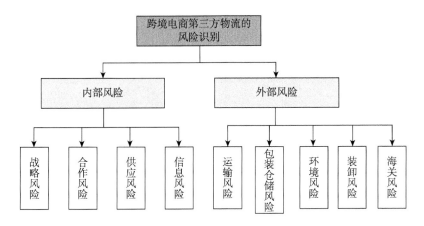

图 3 – 1　跨境电商第三方物流的内部和外部风险识别

Giuffrida 等（2021）认为跨境物流过程中存在 7 类风险：交货风险（delivery uncertainty）、客户服务期待风险（customer service expectation uncertainty）、合规性风险（compliance uncertainty）、外部风险（external uncertainty）、存货管理风险（inventory management uncertainty）、产品或包裹破损（product or parcel damage）等，以及需求预测和管理风险（uncertainty in demand forecasting and management）。这些风险是物流公司在业务运作时必须考虑的风险。企业应根据风险采取相应的策略开展业务。

杨子等（2018）在文献研究的基础上，把跨境电商物流运输的影响因素分为宏观方面和微观方面。宏观方面包括政治、经济、社会、科技等，微观方面为跨境电商企业自身、第三方物流平台、市场和消费者。根据全球跨境电商物流发展方向，遵循规范性、可比性、可操作性和综合性原则，按照层级分析法，构建了跨境电商物流运输的影响因素指标评价三级指标体系。在二级指标层面，作者从信息系统建设、物流系统成本、国际运输质量、运输主体能力、外部环境维护五个方面进行模糊层次分析，结果发现，信息系统建设是最重要的制约因素，其他因素的重要性排序分别是国际运输质量、外部环境维护、运输主体能力、物流系统成本。因此，作者认为物流信息系统建设是跨境物流的重要方面，必须加以重视。在三级指标层面，信息化平台建设、物流技术应用、国际物流法律、第三方物流水平、海关和商检、政策环境、物流管理能力、物流企业规模经营、产品市场状况以及人才的培养等具体方面构成了跨境电商物流供应链发展的制约因素。这些发现也印证了本书第 1 章提及的物流供应链生态系统维护的重要性。因此，作者提出推进跨境物流产业结构性升级、加强物流运输的政策性保障、创新物流企业配送模式，以及提升跨境物流服务质量等建议。这些建议在其他研究中也得到不少回应。

3.2.2 案例研究

高帆（2020）以深圳万邦速达国际物流公司为例展开案例研究，分析中小型跨境物流企业面临的风险，包括物流自身风险、通关风险、交易风险和不可抗力风险四个潜在风险（图 3－2），并为中小物流企业提出了防范对策，如租用或共享海外仓，完善物流信息系统，建立自有清关公司，利用区块链技术进行跨境支付，以及加强对外部风险的防范意识等。

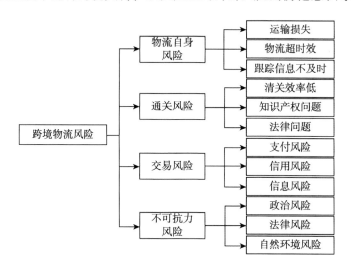

图 3－2　跨境物流风险

针对特殊情况，各风险种类有各自的特点。谢泗薪等（2019）以中美贸易摩擦为背景，分析了跨境电商物流联盟面临的主要内部风险和外部风险。外部风险主要包括一般环境风险、经济环境风险和市场环境风险；内部风险主要包括融资风险、物流能力风险和管理协调能力风险。应对风险的路径是构建创新型跨境电商智慧物流生态系统，三位一体（预测—能力—协调）开展风险防控，是提升我国跨境电商物流联盟抗风险能力的有效举措。赵昕东（2022）以新冠病毒感染疫情后的跨境物流业现状为背景，对跨境电商所面对的物流风险与困境进行分析，认为目前的跨境物流风险主要是以通关为核心的物流风险和以存货为核心的资金风险。

在结合物流模式的风险分析方面，郑小雪等（2016）分析了跨境物流企业面临的风险。她以分析跨境电商物流模式与风险因素为切入点，将可拓模型运用仿真算例中，把两种类型的企业面临的风险指标分为四个等级，并从市场风险、通关风险和运输风险等方面对企业进行风险评估。张铎等（2019）在对跨境物流四种主要模式，即邮政物流、国际快递、海外专线和海外仓综合分析的基础上，采用模糊综合评价法对跨境电商物流模式的风险进行评估和预判。结果表明，七种风险的影响程度有显著差异，对物流风险的防控非常必要。风险防控措施应聚焦完善物流体系，共建物流联盟，提高信息化水平，完善管理机制，防控汇率风险等。

物流联盟是跨境电商物流供应链发展的方向。田青等（2021）研究了当前跨境电商物流联盟模式运作中存在的风险，主要是市场变动风险、运输安全风险、融资风险、物流能力风险和联盟管理风险。基本上可以归为两类，即物流风险和供应链运作风险。杜志平、贡祥林（2018）对跨境物流联盟的风险中的物流运作风险进行了研究，从跨境物流空间跨度大、物流网络复杂、节点变化多等特征出发进行模型研究，进而提出降低风险的外部机制或管理方法。

刘永胜等（2012）针对企业物流风险进行分析，提出企业面临环境风险、市场风险、供应物流风险、生产物流风险、销售物流风险、回收物流风险和整体物流风险七种风险要素，在此基础上，设计并构建了基于企业运作过程的物流风险预警指标体系，并在此基础上做了分析。整体来看，现有研究还存在一些有待完善之处，跨境物流联盟面临的物流风险可以通过建立物流风险的预警机制体系提前防范，从而降低风险带来的成本，但物流风险的防范及规避取决于物流联盟链条的平稳运行效率，因此，供应链联盟的合作风险才是跨境物流联盟面临的主要风险（杜志平，2018）。物流联盟的合作风险决定了物流联盟能否稳定正常运行，只有进行有效的风险管理，建立合理的利益分配机制，强化价值共同创造机制，才能更好地提升跨境物流联盟的稳定性。

江旭、姜飞飞（2015）的研究围绕交易成本理论进行分析，认为联盟具有外部不确定性，分别为环境不确定性与伙伴行为不确定性。研究表明，企业对联盟风险的有效管理能够提高物流联盟合作绩效的满意度。李实萍等（2014）通过对两个航空公司组成的航空联盟的研究，发现实施共享机制可以实现联盟成员的效益最大化。周敏、黄福华（2013）从物流联盟运作特点出发，利用博弈论分析了物流联盟各成员的行为模式，探讨了合作风险分担方案，以及该方案的合理性和稳定性，提出建立风险公益金制度，以解决跨境物流联盟风险共担的问题。

综上所述，跨境的物流风险主要体现在图 3 - 3。

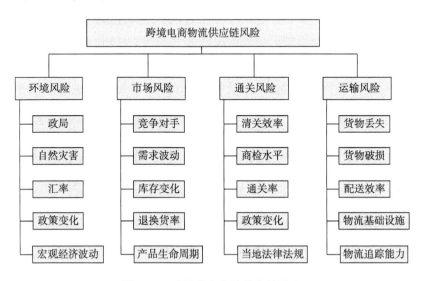

图 3 - 3　跨境电商物流供应链风险

3.3　海外仓风险评估

目前，我国海外仓经营面临的主要风险是经营风险和决策风险。海外仓作为新型物流模式对解决我国目前出口贸易中面临的诸多实际运营风险，如时效性差、售后效率低、物流费用高、库存不精准等问题有显著作用。在此背景下，国内外学者从不同角度对海外仓经营中面临的风险做了广泛研究。曹倩、蒋晶（2022）认为，目前海外仓企业面临的主要风险是法律政策风险、市场风险、管理风险和成本风险等。周广澜、范志颖（2021）利用系统动力学建模，探究了海外仓服务对跨境电商出口交易的影响。他们通过敏感性分析认为，对于海外仓服务影响最大的是通关风险，因此，跨境物流企业在分配海外仓各项业务投入时可倾向于清关环节。郭文强、王彦博（2022）分析了亚马逊物流配送、自建海外仓和第三方海外仓三种海外仓模式，认为三种海外仓模式适合不同类型和发展阶段的企业。因此，不同企业应结合自身特点选择适合自己的海外仓。方思（2020）提出海外仓种类的选择直接关系到海外仓经营效率风险的高低，因此，在"人货场"海外仓选择策略上，建议企业可根据自身发展情况、产品类型及消费地区特点，判断适合的海外仓模式。海外仓本质上作为一种资本密集型和技术密集型产业，需要大量的资金和人力投入。而资金问题和人才匮乏是当前大部分跨境电商企业面临的风险问题。对此，陶正（2021）提出，企业可以依托产业集群，建立跨境电商企业联盟，并在此基础上通过协议、合资、入股等方式共建海外仓，且企业要通过建立海外仓风险预警机制来抵御海外仓风险。权印（2020）基于共享经济思维，提出建立共享海外仓的方法，通过建立海外仓综合服务平台，实现海外仓资源与信息的有效共享。

海外仓的出现大大推动了跨境电商的进一步发展，但海外仓经营中面临的风险也是境内仓的倍数级，对海外仓风险的控制和规避策略将在本书第 5 章中详细探讨。

3.4　宏观风险评估

除了对跨境物流风险微观层面的分析和评估，很多学者还关注到了影响跨境物流发展的宏观层面。但相对于跨境物流风险的微观研究而言，关注我国跨境电商宏观环境的研究相对较少。

第一，跨境物流供应链政策方面，基于PEST理论的跨境电商宏观环境研究相对比较成熟。郭燕等（2020）运用PEST宏观环境分析模型，从政治（P）、经济（E）、社会（S）、技术（T）四个方面分析我国跨境电商所处的宏观竞争环境。我国的跨境物流供应链宏观政策的颁布经历了两个阶段，分别是2013年起的中央集中立法阶段和各省市区域立法阶段。在政策内容方面，政府着重倾听了企业的需求，要建立与数字贸易相适应的跨境电商制度标准。研究建议应搭建更多的平台，为中小企业获取有效的信息创造途径。政府应确保政策符合本地的区域发展特点，推进符合当地特点的精准贸易政策。

熊励、叶凯雯（2020）从政策角度提出了跨境电商生态系统，分析了跨境电商生态发展与跨境电商政策的关联性，提出"生态系统—政策组合"跨境电商政策分析框架（图3－4）。他们把政策工具组合分为四类：环境型（占比74.51%）、供给型（占比14.52%）、需求型（占比2.9%）、评估型（占比8.06%），四类政策工具相互配合，通过"形—推—拉—评"的共同作用推进跨境电商生态的健康发展。国家层面的跨境电商政策中，环境型政策工具使用数量最多，其次为供给型和评估型政策工具，需求型政策工具严重缺位。他们认为，现有政策对跨境电商生态体系的影响已经深入支付、税收、监管、物流、信息化等领域，但跨境电商人才、知识产权保护等内容依然有所欠缺。在需求型政策工具严重缺位的情况下，需要从政策层面对国际合作、税收政策、扩大出口与内需等方面加强引导，刺激消费需求。此外，宏观政策在整个跨境物流生态系统中融入度不够，政府仍然没有实现从监管到支撑的角色转变。

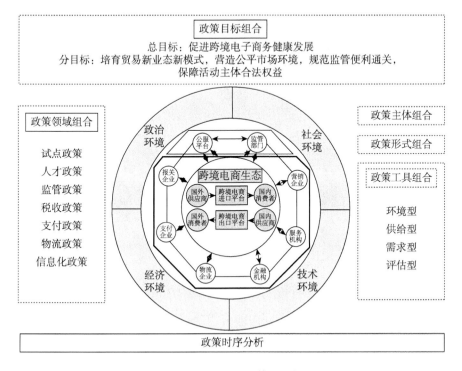

图 3 - 4　跨境电商政策分析框架

　　第二，制度距离和文化距离方面，多数研究围绕国家间经济、政治、法律、文化等制度环境的差异进行。学者们围绕如何细化制度距离展开研究，有些学者在细化制度距离时，也融入了文化距离，认为文化差异代表的文化距离也是造成制度距离的因素之一。另外一些学者在制度距离中加入了政策因素，Estrin 等（2009）区分了正式和非正式的制度距离，前者包括法律条文、商业惯例等，后者包括文化习俗、价值观念、社会信仰等。而制度距离合并文化距离以及地理距离，都被认为是跨境电商和跨境物流供应链发展的阻碍因素。

　　李元旭、罗佳（2017）从消费者角度出发，使用文化距离和制度距离理论分析跨境电商中的风险。制度距离又分为经济制度和法治制度两个方面。一般使用遗产基金会、华尔街时报和加拿大弗雷泽研究所公布的各年度"经济自由度指数"来衡量经济制度。而法治制度的度量使用"全球治理指标"（Worldwide Governance Indicators，WGI）来衡量。基于所得到的各个国家的经济制度和法治制度的数据，构建国家之间的制度距离。他们借鉴了西方学者的风险分类，用五个维度来度量消费者感知到的风险（perceived risk）：（1）卖方风险，指电商卖家为追求利益最大化而产生的有损害顾客利益的行为；（2）产品风险，指消费者对产品在质量、性能等方面达不到预期效果的担心；（3）经济风险，指网购可能引起财务损失或额外花费的担心；（4）配送风险，指因送货造成产品破损或丢失的担心；（5）个人信息被滥用风险，指个人信息可能被盗取、滥用的担心。根据这五个维度，编制了测量题项。他们使用权力距离维度、个人主义维度、不确定性规避维度和男性主义维度四个文化维度来测量文化距离。研究结果表明，文化距离对五个维度的跨境电商风险均呈现显著性，经济制度距离显著影响消费者的卖方风险、经济风险和个人信息滥用风险。相比之下，法治制度距离对产品风险没有影响，但过大的法治制度距离会对其他四个风险构成影响。经济制度的差异不但对跨境电商产生影响，对服务贸易出口竞争力也会产生较大的影响（宋津睿、崔日明，2021）。因此，从制度距离和文化距离角度进行优化也是跨境物流供应链优化的必然选择。

第4章　跨境电商物流供应链的优化

本章基于跨境电商生态系统，从宏观和微观两个方面展开跨境物流供应链的优化，以此促进跨境电商的长期、健康、可持续发展。

跨境物流供应链生态系统精细而复杂，跨越不同的国家，连接不同的行业，整合不同的运输方式，任何环节的风险都有可能造成跨境电商交易成本的增加或效率的降低，甚至是交易失败，因此，对跨境物流生态系统进行优化是长期的内在要求。

4.1　宏观优化

跨境电商物流生态系统是由外部环境塑造的。本书第 3 章分析了跨境电商物流供应链的宏观风险，本章将在分析风险和问题的基础上，提出跨境物流宏观层面的优化方案。在数字经济的大背景下，宏观层面的优化要以缩短贸易距离、数字距离和制度距离为原则。

为了实现这一目标，需要考虑贸易政策、数字基础设施以及消费者行为模式等多方面因素。宏观环境的优化还需要解决跨境法规、数字化和标准化、环保低碳供应链等方面存在的问题。

通过改善宏观环境，跨境电商物流将变得更高效、更灵活、更安全，从而支持该行业的可持续发展。此外，这也将推动创新并促进数字化和传统业务的整合，为跨境贸易创造更有利的环境。

4.1.1 优化原则

4.1.1.1 缩短贸易距离

地理距离、制度距离和文化距离因素构成贸易距离，它们都对跨境电商贸易发展产生阻力。唐红涛、朱梦琦（2021）将这三个因素统一称为贸易成本。跨境物流的优化以降本增效为目的，因此，缩短贸易距离也是跨境物流降本的一部分。互联网技术已经从实际意义上帮助跨境电商企业跨越了地理距离，大大降低了跨境电商与地理距离相关的贸易成本。文化的差异非一朝一夕能改变，需要深层次和多频次的沟通才能在一定程度上缩短文化距离。而跨境电商刻意设计的优化政策可以达到缩短文化距离的目的。例如，跨境电商平台提供多种语言的服务支持，便能够降低沟通成本，提高交易效率，弱化文化差异。

4.1.1.2 缩短制度距离

此处的制度距离，也是贸易距离的范畴，在此单独论述。缩短制度距离并非简单的措施可以实现，尤其在当前全球经济局势下，跨境电商发展面临贸易保护主义、逆全球化趋势、贸易摩擦的干扰，这些正是制度距离的本质体现。唐红涛、朱梦琦（2021）将跨境电商范畴中制度距离的重点放在经济制度上，认为弱化制度距离其实是缩短经济制度距离。因此，跨境电商和跨境物流的发展与制度距离的缩短互为因果。促进各国政府合作，在商业惯例、交易流程等方面达成一致，对跨境电商中制度差异的弱化具有重要作用。

经济制度具体指的是各个国家和地区在国际经济规则、知识产权保护、个人隐私保护、数据传输等方面的不同政策。政策的差异必然限制了跨境电商和跨境物流的顺畅进行。缩小与目的国家之间的距离，在经济制度上实现衔接、对接、接轨和改善，才是弱化经济制度距离的关键。就我国跨境电商和跨境物流的制度体系而言，中国的跨境物流发展仍处在初级阶段。由于发展时间较短，法规体系仍然不健全。一些国内相关规则和国际规则不能无缝对接，有些规则和国际规则冲突，当然还有些相应的法规缺失，法规体系仍然有很大的发展空间。因此，从缩短制度距离的角度，应做好以下两点。第一，努力缩小与发达国家在经济制度和法律制度上的差距，提高中国产品在这些国家的认同度，有助于降低风险，提高与这些国家的消费者达成交易的概率。第二，通过实现国内政策和国际政策的协调、衔接、接轨、调整，在政府部门的协调下，主动降低贸易摩擦和壁垒，通过推动产业政策、贸易政策和竞争政策的协调，建立更公平的全球市场环境，真正实现与国际市场的接轨（蒲新蓉，2022）。

4.1.1.3　缩短数字距离

随着数字技术在跨境电商中的重要性日益凸显，"数字距离"的概念逐步形成。数字距离一般是指不同国家、地区、企业由于信息基础设施、拥有网络技术的程度差异所造成的国家与国家之间、地区与地区之间、企业与企业之间数字技术发展距离逐渐拉大的现象。这种发展的不均衡造成全球供应链信息不通畅、数据不共享和流程不协调等问题，从而形成数字隔阂，最终导致物流过程的效率低、成本增加、客户体验降低等问题。杨继军等（2022）将数字距离描述为"数字鸿沟"，由依托数字基础设施、连接互联网的"接入鸿沟"，掌握数字技术知识、应用数字技术的"使用鸿沟"，以及获取数据资源、创造数据财富的"能力鸿沟"三个部分组成。而"鸿沟"一词的使用本身就代表着数字距离之大，短时间内难以跨越。且数字产业链的发展容易呈现马太效应，强者愈强，而弱者愈弱。

发展中国家数字基础设施发展相对落后，缺乏良好的数字贸易发展环境，限制了其参与全球产业链、供应链分工的广度和深度。数字经济大国在数字接入上的优势，容易触发数字产业链的正反馈机制，呈现出强者愈强的现象。目前，全球 80% 的数据被发达国家控制，核心技术的掌握情况更是如此，这对发展中国家数字经济的发展制约很大。

4.1.2 优化策略

跨境电商物流供应链生态系统包括政治、经济、社会、技术、环境和法规六大因素，跨境电商宏观优化政策可从这六个方面入手。首先，增加政治经济方面的合作沟通。而沟通的前提是文化上的互通互认，因此，增加文化的认同感能够为进一步的经济合作打下坚实的基础。其次，政府推动跨境平台的数字化建设，完善相关领域的规范化运行，为平台的数字化转型提供良好的环境。最后，在碳达峰和碳中和的大目标指引下，政府和企业应共同努力保证跨境供应链的绿色低碳发展。这些宏观优化政策共同发力，可以为跨境电商物流供应链的整合和一体化提供强力支撑，促进跨境电商健康发展。

4.1.2.1 增加社会文化认同

政府除了予以跨境电子商务企业政策上的支持，还应当在国家层面进行全球范围的文化传播，让中国文化融入世界文化，在保留中国文化特色的同时，提高中国文化的国际认同。在文化沟通的基础上，进一步打通交易双方贸易沟通的通道，加强与各国之间的合作，以树立我国在国际商贸沟通中的友好形象，吸引更多国家与我们进行合作，提升海外用户对我国产品的信任度（李元旭、罗佳，2017）。

4.1.2.2 推动数字化赋能

数字经济赋能跨境物流是未来发展的趋势。数字基础设施作为信息的基本通道，发挥着大动脉的作用，是发展高质量跨境物流的关键支撑。推动数字经济发展，重在健全数字经济相关的法律法规，完善数字经济治理，引导平台经济经营者依法合规经营，维护公平有序的市场竞争环境，实现大数据支撑下的政策制定和制度衔接。

4.1.2.3 发展低碳物流和供应链

"双碳"目标下，我国的对外贸易面临巨大挑战。世界各国陆续提出了自己的碳达峰、碳中和目标，国内外"双碳"目标对我国跨境电商的发展也会产生不小的影响。中国政府和企业不仅需要尽快在短期内加速转变经贸和物流供应链结构，还需要应对国际压力，尤其是发达国家的碳壁垒、碳关税以及复杂的贸易政策。承担应尽的碳减排义务、实行低碳经济发展，相应地推进跨境电商和物流的低碳化发展（王晓煜等，2021）的目标对我国环境保护的理念、实践、政策和法规等都是不小的挑战。例如，快时尚跨境电商希音公司靠优质的物流供应链取得了巨大的成功，同时公司也承受极大的社会责任、环境责任的压力。[①] 环境问题成为快时尚行业最受非议的部分。

4.1.2.4 完善法律法规

为了推动跨境电子商务的发展，我国政府制定了相应的扶持政策，例如，国务院办公厅 2015 年印发的《关于促进跨境电子商务健康快速发展的指导意见》、2022 年印发的《"十四五"现代物流发展规划》在政策层面对中国跨境电子商务的发展起到了推动作用。李益帆、陈娟（2022）从三个方面讨论了国内跨境物流行业的规范，一是可以通过健全行业标准，营造一个良好的港航物流氛围；二是需要对垄断、倒卖和恶意订舱等不法行为依法进行严厉的打击处罚，稳定航运费用；三是积极推进跨境物流国内段的规范管理，推动各级、各地方政府各监管部门之间的有效沟通和协作，加强政府监管。三个方面的规范政策旨在形成跨境电商发展的总体布局，再辅以税费优惠政策或政府财政补贴等相关政策优惠。如在疫情期间，政府通过法规和建议等给予了中小型企业更大力度的扶持政策，帮助他们顺利渡过了难关，强化了企业的抗风险能力，也利于推动跨境电商行业未来的高质量发展。

我国现有的跨境电商国内规则框架不够完善，参与国际跨境电商规则的力度不大，只在少数几个双边和区域贸易协定中辟有电子商务专章。数

---

① 希音. "超快时尚"的 ESG 原罪［EB/OL］.（2022 - 07 - 21）［2023 - 04 - 28］. ht-tps：//baijiahao. baidu. com/s？id = 1738958743073736548&wfr = spider&for = pc.

字经济的快速发展，推动我国跨境电商规则更多地关注无形的数字产品和服务贸易，相关知识产权、税收规则也应该扩大调整范围。此外，跨境电商贸易与网络安全的关系也需要重新界定。尽管欧美国家跨境电商及数字贸易规则较为成熟，但我国应制定符合国情的国际贸易和物流规则。在借鉴国外贸易规则的基础上，我国应从顶层设计、国内规则制定、国际规则参与、双边及区域谈判实践等方面不断完善跨境电商物流供应链规则（陈志娟，2021）。

综上所述，宏观方面，我国现代商贸物流体系在政策红利的引导下，开始了初步的发展，基本形成了规模，奠定了未来良好发展的基础。政府在推出支持政策的同时，须深入研究企业的实际经营状况，做到政策关注实际问题，解决企业实际经营困难。

4.2 微观优化

跨境电商物流供应链是个复杂的系统，除了以上论述的宏观层面的复杂性，还涉及跨境电商平台、跨境物流平台、国内供应链平台和跨境支付等方面，包括供应商、制造商、分销商、零售商和消费者等跨境电商主体。总体来说，跨境物流供应链企业的整体能力主要体现在信息能力、物流能力和资金能力三个方面，构成物流供应链三大支柱。本部分将从这三个角度出发，探讨如何通过跨境物流数字化优化方案提升跨境物流的信息能力，通过跨境物流集群化优化方案提升跨境物流的物流能力和资金能力，在此基础上，围绕数字经济和物流联盟两个核心主题，提出我国跨境电商物流发展模式的优化方案。

4.2.1 数字经济赋能跨境物流供应链

跨境电商物流供应链企业的信息能力与数字经济密切相关。企业需不断提高其信息化的能力。通过数字经济的发展，企业的信息化能力得到提升，从而增强跨境电商供应链的柔性和韧性，全面提升其抗风险的能力。

数字经济是以使用数字化的知识和信息作为关键生产要素，以现代信息网络作为重要载体，以通信技术的有效使用作为效率提升和经济结构优化的重要推动力的一系列经济活动。发展数字经济意义重大，是把握新一轮科技革命和产业变革新机遇的战略选择。数字技术对经济发展具有放大、叠加、倍增的作用。我国数字经济发展规模位居世界前列。其中，产业数字化是数字经济发展的重要特征。2022 年 3 月 28 日，中国国际经济交流中心发布的《数字平台助力中小企业参与全球供应链竞争》报告称，数字化国际供应链时代正加速到来。当前，数字平台运用大数据、云计算、虚拟现实等新一代数字化智能技术，集成外贸供应链各环节数据，形成新业态驱动、大数据支撑、网络化共享、智能化协作的供应链体系，从而在更大范围内形成了数字驱动的新型供应链和价值链。本书第 3 章对跨境物流不同模式的物流风险进行了风险识别和评估。跨境物流级别较高的风险主要是运输风险、通关风险和稳定性风险。数字化供应链将有助于降低这三种主要风险。

4.2.1.1　数字经济赋能供应链风险控制

随着大数据、云计算、人工智能等新一代数字技术的渗透，全球供应链呈现"数字化""智能化""网络化"趋势。以大数据为核心进行预测、评估并生成供应链解决方案，可推动跨境供应链韧性增强，更加灵活地应对跨境运输风险、通关风险和市场风险。具体表现在以下三个方面。

首先，数字技术赋能供应链应对运输风险。数字技术通过平台直接将供给方与需求方进行对接，压缩了众多中间环节，实现了供应链的扁平化发展，环节的减少提升了供应链的整体顺畅运行。数字技术促进了供应链的分工细化，节约了成本。通过推动跨境电商供应链的成本节约效应和出口增值效应来重塑分工形态，进而推动供应链的功能互补和协同。具体而言，数字技术通过渗入产业链、供应链的各个环节，贯穿从生产端到流通端，再到最终消费端，实现了货、人、钱、道、仓、运具等要素的数字化高效精准匹配（杨继军等，2022）。在此过程中，数字技术收集散落在供应链各环节中离散的数据，帮助物流企业有效处理大数据并对供应链环节的网络进行动态优化，帮助企业有效开拓大数据应用途径（马述忠、郭继文，2020）。不但可降低交易成本，而且可提前预测运输环节风险，提升供应链的抗风险韧性。无论是这些研究中提到的分工更专业化，还是流程的扁平化、智能化，都体现了数字技术赋能跨境电商供应链，提升供应链韧性。

其次，数字技术赋能供应链应对通关风险。通关业务属于跨境电商生态系统的支持物种，在电商生态系统中起到承上启下的作用。建立在数字化技术基础之上的平台，能够实现报关报检、出口清关、税收结算等功能，由海关、政府和相关企业进行管理建设，实现信息的统一交换和传递。运用数字化技术，实现通关的无纸化，简化通关手续降低通关风险，是物流供应链提高效率的重要环节。

最后，数字技术赋能全球供应链的稳定性。供应链顾名思义是一个互相咬合的链条，链条中的任何一个企业受到外部冲击而停止运营都会影响到供应链的整体运营。近年来，由于新冠病毒感染疫情的影响，供应链延迟，甚至中断的情况比比皆是。以数字技术赋能的数字化跨境供应链能够更好地实现供应链柔化，提升供应链韧性，形成"链—图—策"全景动态的供应链模式（杨继军等，2022）。"数字化"供应链可以实现线下到线上的灵活转换。当线下供应链受到冲击时，数字化供应链能够及时将线下需求转移到线上，进而提高全球供应链的灵活性和稳定性。

4.2.1.2　物流供应链的数字化优化策略

数字技术赋能我国跨境供应链的低成本高效率运转。跨境电商物流行业提升数字化水平是突破行业瓶颈和实现供应链降本增效的必然选择，也是打造集干线运输、仓储服务、配送服务、售后服务、销售预测、库存管理等服务于一体的智慧物流系统的基础（李益帆、陈娟，2022）。整个供应链各环节在数字技术的加持下，共同配合，实现最优价值链。

首先，实现跨境物流供应链的标准化。

跨境物流数字化的前提是实现物流供应链标准化。以跨境物流的时效性为例，由于涉及多方主体，所以对每一环节的时间节点，都需要制定一个明确的标准才能使整个供应链流程衔接顺畅。除时间节点的标准化，标识的标准化、流程的标准化同样关系到数字化和集成化的实现，例如，一个跨境包裹由国内发往海外，跨境物流的每一道环节中都有不同单位参与，因此，每个包裹至少需要贴上 7～8 个标签。如果这些标签不能被准确识别，那么境内外的物流很难连接顺畅。

其次，充分发挥平台整合优势。

在整合思维的指导下，利用综合平台的整合和集成效应，可以降低跨境物流运输成本，降低运输风险，提高物流效率，是物流供应链发展的大方向。

建设综合物流服务平台，对卖方订单数据进行评估，预测所需物流资源，然后对接物流公司的物流供给数据，进行双向数据整合，借鉴共享经济概念，实现物流供需双方的信息对接。这样就可以利用上述平台信息集聚的优势，为卖方提供集装箱拼箱等集约化的物流方式，以降低跨境物流运输成本，提高物流运输效率，降低集装箱空置率，实现物流运输集约化，为跨境物流提供低成本的运输方案。因此，物流平台企业需要提升整体的系统化、信息化建设，利用高新技术对数据进行收集、分析、得出结果，并实时将货物的物理移动转化为电子信息的流动，实现"货物—运力—信息"的无缝对接和匹配。能够实现这样操作的综合平台需要做到高度信息透明化。信息透明化主要体现为价格透明，平台通过打通物流公司与跨境卖家间壁垒，使用户可以在平台上询价，以提供付费参考。通俗地说，这类平台更像是跨境物流领域中的"携程"。

此外，为了提升客户体验和信任度，平台的物流信息系统应做可视化处理，为卖家和客户提供真实可查、全程跟踪的货物信息，及时反馈解决运输问题，减少货物运输时间，保证货物运输的安全性，提升客户的信任感和体验感。可视化的核心在于通过平台实现物流追踪，将全链条各个节点可视化，使得原本的黑箱运输无所遁形。

最后，利用先进技术完善供应链流程。

跨境电商物流供应链是先进技术和设备的天然试验场，如运用人工智能等先进技术，探索智慧物流供应链的配送模式，可以大幅度降低物流成本，降低市场风险，提高供应链效率。

目前，跨境电商平台运用人工智能（Artificial Intelligence，AI）、区块链（blockchain）、射频识别（Radio Frequency Identification，RFID）等先进技术集成跨境电商物流链条上各产品、各服务商的数据，建立起具有物流数据管理功能的数字化作业系统。例如，"运去哪"平台（https：//www. yunquna. com/）目前通过人工智能、自然语言处理（Natural Language Processing，NLP）、知识图谱、机器人流程自动化（Robotic Process Automation，RPA）等算法能力，来提升行业的履约效率。并且已经可以提供包括港区、箱货、船期、拖车定位、船计划、船舶定位、编码协调制度、拖车费用、内装费用、报关费用、海运保险费用等在内的查询体系。[①] 跨境电商平台还应积极推进无人机配送、智能快递柜和城市物流综合平台的研发与应用，切实完成"最后一公里"的及时配送，构建海外市场的智慧物流配送新模式。除头程和尾程的技术应用，跨境电商企业也要充分利用数字技术，实现网络化、智能化、精准化的信息，并做到与前端销售实时同步，作为物流系统的指导信息。物流企业需要充分了解货物目的国的经济情况、促销时间、货物销售趋势等信息，利用智慧物流信息系统精准判断市场，准确预测库存信息，有针对性地进行配货补货，从而避免缺货或者囤积的情况。

不论是传统物流，还是跨境物流，都是一个不断集散的过程，而不同环节的集散，以环节的标准化为前提，以综合性的物流平台为基础，以先进的技术为支撑，来完成跨境物流的一体化集成。

---

① 潘潇雨. 跨境物流行业红利已过，数字化拐点将至 | 焦点分析 ［EB/OL］. （2021 – 10 – 29）［2023 – 4 – 28］. https：//baijiahao. baidu. com/s？id =1714940607259323575&wfr = spider&for = pc.

4.2.2　跨境物流供应链的一体化集成

从第 3 章对跨境物流联盟的风险评估和讨论可见，跨境电商物流服务资源分散、市场集中度低，海外仓等资源共享程度低，供应链中高端服务和增值能力较弱，构成阻碍我国跨境电商发展的显著因素。要改变这一现状，需要整合各方资源、优势互补，形成全球化物流网络、提高跨境电商物流整体服务绩效的新型组织运作模式，即物流联盟。我国企业如何构建跨境物流联盟，实现国际化物流运营体系，成为我国物流业发展迫切需要解决的当务之急。

4.2.2.1　物流联盟

物流联盟是为了帮助会员物流企业获得单独从事物流活动所无法获得的更好效果，在企业间形成相互信任、共担风险、共享收益的物流伙伴关系（田宇、朱道立，2000；杜志平，2020）。这种联盟是参与各方基于在物流领域的战略性协作框架下开展有组织的市场交易，一方面有利于节约跨境电商市场交易中的相关成本，另一方面有利于提高各方对环境不确定性的应变能力，降低由此带来的经营风险（李旭东等，2017）。作为适应新形势的跨境电商物流形态，跨境物流联盟的重要特点之一就是，它通常是围绕某一国家的核心企业建立并运行的。

4.2.2.2　我国跨境物流联盟的发展阶段

李旭东等（2017）将跨境电商物流企业联盟总结为三种类型，即该联盟发展的三个阶段。首先是初级阶段，在这个阶段物流联盟由大型 3PL 企业主导。发展势头好的 3PL 企业整合其他 3PL 企业资源向 4PL 转型，并向其跨境物流客户提供整合的物流服务。第二阶段为中级阶段，物流联盟由比较成熟的 4PL 企业或大型跨境电商平台主导。主导企业设立综合性平台，提供全方位平台化服务，如采购、仓储、运输、通关、包装、配送、售后服务等服务功能，整合跨境电商供应链各环节资源，为整个跨境电供应链提供全程服务。第三阶段为高级阶段，物流联盟由全球化4PL集团主导。这种跨境物流联盟突破了单一产业供应链的覆盖范围，实现产业跨界，并在全球范围内整合跨境电商供应链，在联盟成员间建立合理的利益分配机制，实现互利共赢，提升跨境电商物流效率与服务水平，并能够切实降低综合物流成本，是跨境物流联盟的最高形式。

当前，我国的跨境物流联盟正处于第二阶段。如阿里巴巴作为核心企业，已经构建了一个综合性跨境物流平台，整合了各种跨境电商供应链资源，为客户提供一条龙的跨境电商服务。阿里巴巴正在努力将联盟向第三阶段发展。然而，由于国情的特殊性，我国也已经基本形成了一个由政府主导的跨境电商4PL联盟机制。这种机制主要集中在跨境电商试点城市，并由政府牵头在自贸区搭建了专门的平台作为跨境物流生态圈的核心。为了打造国际物流中心，政府还设立了跨境电商产业园区，并将生态圈的关键物种和支撑物种类型集中在一起，包括涉及关检、金融、咨询等机构，甚至还有外围物种机构，形成了一个跨境电商供应链服务一体化的物流联盟生态。

从上述跨境物流联盟发展阶段可以看出，在跨境物流生态系统中处于核心位置的是跨境物流联盟，以核心企业为中心，打造开放式供应链生态系统，为物流供应链中的每个参与者提供相关的支持服务，参与者协同为客户提供个性化的高端物流服务，见图4-1（李旭东等，2017）。

跨境物流联盟在跨境物流生态系统中处于核心位置，也是跨境物流生态系统实现降本增效、协同发展的关键。跨境物流联盟是企业的集群。在合作优势理论之下，企业集群能够带来相应的合作绩效，形成规模经济，达到降本增效的目的。

从企业内部来看，物流联盟的优势体现在以下四个方面。

（1）物流联盟的形成，可促进内部分工更加专业化。同国际贸易的比较优势理论基础相似，在细化分工的基础上，企业分工与合作能够增加资源的利用率，减少资源重复和浪费，达到"降本"的目的。

（2）通过物流联盟成员的合作，可以精简重复设置的机构，经过精简的机构运转效率更高，可达到"增效"的目的。

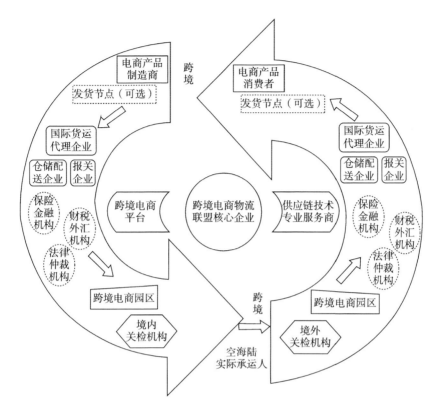

图 4 - 1　基于 4PL 的跨境电商物流联盟组织机制

（3）经过长期的稳定合作，物流联盟内部可形成稳定的组织结构。联盟成员之间相互依赖，合作共赢，这种稳定的协作机制和信任机制能够有效地避免逆向选择和道德风险，使得物流联盟的稳定性大大增强。

（4）物流联盟可提升市场竞争力。稳定运转的物流联盟实现降本增效之后，提升的市场竞争力必定使它们拥有更多的低价使用物流资源的机会，能够以较低的市场价格获得更多的市场资源，产生更好的联盟扩张效应。

从外部环境来看，物流联盟的优势体现在以下三个方面。

（1）通过建立物流联盟，实现规模经济，低价寻求外部资源，降本增效。跨境电商物流联盟模式的高效运作，可有效降低联盟运营成本。而这一目标的实现，离不开配套基础设施的支持与服务。近年来，在政府相关部门的支持下，中国跨境电商物流基础设施逐渐完善，跨境电商物流联盟模式运营成本不断下降。

（2）物流联盟的形成可以让成员企业通过联合行动扩大市场份额，提高市场容量。通过物流联盟的资源整合和协同合作，企业可以更快速地进入新的市场，开展跨境业务，获得更多的订单和收入。在市场规模扩大的同时，企业能够更好地分担市场风险，提高市场竞争力。

（3）跨境物流联盟的组合能够更好地利用国内和国外两个市场中的资源。在更广阔的空间中实现资源配置，瞄准全球市场的资源，实现全球范围内的资源配置。

4.2.2.3 跨境物流联盟的优化策略

目前我国的跨境物流联盟尚处于中级阶段向高级阶段的发展过程中。联盟成员之间难以形成稳定的协同管理体系，成员之间利益冲突大，利益难以协调，主要是因为组织中缺乏核心企业或机构能够平衡各成员之间的利益关系，联盟成员间的摩擦不断。即便勉强维持联盟关系，也很难共同合作实现战略性目标。且组织成员的加入随机性大，组织结构松散，联盟成员之间缺乏必要的信息共享和沟通机制，联盟集群难以实现稳定长期发展。因此，我国跨境物流联盟的优化方案，应从优化物流联盟的顶层设计方案开始。

在物流联盟的顶层优化策略上，江运芳（2022）建议设立类似"跨境物流管理局"的管理机构。可通过"中央＋地方"的立体式扶持网络，对跨境电商物流联盟内的相关企业进行管理和扶持。

中央设立管理机构后，地方政府牵头与企业接洽，通过企业注资、政府扶持等方式，建立专业化集成化的地方产业园区，推动地方跨境物流集散中心的建设，形成特色化的区域产业集群化。例如，2022年底，中国建立了锡盟空港物流园区，包括产权交易平台、机动车检测服务平台与物流信息化平台。在政府协调下，规划实施快递物流产业中心、多式联运中心。该园区目前已实现跨境电商冷链运输、物流配送与商贸流通，区域内跨境电商物流基础设施集成度提升，形成的跨境电商物流联盟运输成本较初期至少降低 30%。2012 年，鄂尔多斯空港物流园区建立，该产业园区是集临空临港、综合保税、加工制造、现代物流、电子商务等功能于一体的自治区级重点产业园区。2021 年，实现销售收入 22.1 亿元，成为现代物流服务业集成化的良好示范。

"中央 + 地方"扶持模式有利于解决跨境电商的国内发展问题，但是跨境物流联盟还涉及跨境的问题，政府还应该加强与外国政府的经济合作常态化机制的磋商，主要针对目前较为常见的关税和贸易壁垒等贸易争端问题的解决，推动国际贸易跨越国别顺利开展。同时也要防止贸易形势突变给跨境电商物流联盟带来的负面影响，以实际行动消除或者缩短制度距离。

在政府政策保障基础上，物流联盟内部也要实现管理能力的提升。首先，物流联盟要打造创新型跨境物流联盟综合服务平台。跨境电商物流生态系统的核心就是跨境物流联盟打造的一个具有自动化、信息化运营能力的综合服务平台。跨境电商物流联盟应借助跨境综合服务平台，提供专业化跨境服务，实现降本增效。持续改进跨境物流联盟内部运作模式的创新，打造创新型的"互联网跨境物流 +"模式下高效运作的综合服务平台。

例如，早在 2019 年初，京东物流下设的京东云仓就已经开始筹划云物流平台的搭建，为境外合作方提供"物流 + 商流"解决方案，降低仓储成本，同时提升了跨境电商物流的运输水平、货物处理与容纳能力，通过以平台为基础的物流联盟模式实现了跨境物流的降本增效。2019 年 1 月 3 日，派维（Parcelway）跨境供应链综合服务平台与深圳速必达、希杰、云速供应链管理和乐丰联运、网易速达等多家物流企业签约，共同打造形成多主体参与的运作模式。这些合作标志着跨境电商物流联盟的发展进入了一个新的阶段。通过与多家物流企业的合作，派维跨境供应链综合服务平台能够更好地满足消费者对物流服务的需求，提高物流配送效率，降低物流成本。

新冠病毒感染疫情带来了跨境电商的大发展。2022 年末，随着全球新冠病毒感染疫情趋于结束，跨境电商产业的发展迎来了调整和业绩的下滑。2021 年 4 月，亚马逊大规模封号。2022 年 PayPal 向独立站卖家启动了"资金清零"政策。美国商标局制裁上万个中国商标。中国到美国西部海运价格暴跌，仍然"一船难满"。同时，美国 DTC 领头羊股价集体跳水，亚马逊、阿里巴巴、字节跳动等头部公司大规模裁员、业务优化、战略收缩。再如，加拿大电商平台和服务商 Shopify 裁员，股价下跌，京东、东南亚电商平台 Shopee 等电商平台国际化业务扩展受挫，跨境物流供应链也面临严峻挑战。2022 年，跨境电商充满了不确定性，国际物流供应链也随之剧烈波动，不少物流供应链公司面临倒闭。国际供应链后疫情时代的发展有望从 2019 年的状态重新出发。未来几年将更加依赖其自身的内生动力来实现结构优化，顺利渡过全球经济下滑，实现新的、更大的发展。

其次，物流联盟内部推进核心技术的应用，打造数字跨境联盟体系。

在物流联盟内部运用智慧物流核心技术，应用精准包裹追踪系统智能化、数字化技术，实现跨境电商物流联盟模式运作环节的可视化追踪，降低运输安全风险。我国的跨境电商物流联盟应积极寻求相匹配的国内外智慧技术，提升模式运作效率。近年来，中国跨境电商物流企业先后引入了诸多新兴技术，有效提升了跨境电商物流联盟模式的数字化程度，降低了运营成本，提高了物流效率。例如，阿里巴巴收购东南亚最大电商平台 Lazada，自建"Lazada 钱包 + 货到付款"支付体系，实现了跨境网购与支付的高效对接。

跨境物流联盟运用核心技术，打造数字跨境联盟体系。在大数据的加持之下，能够更好地兼顾到中小型跨境电商企业，体察其需求，为其提供个性化的支持服务。随着越来越多的中小微企业开展跨境电商物流业务，跨境物流综合服务的需求快速扩大。跨境物流综合服务企业依托信息技术和资源整合优势，推进跨境物流流程标准化和信息化，为中小企业提供通关、税收、结汇、物流、信保、融资等环节一体化专业服务（曲维玺、王惠敏，2021），提升其跨境物流效率，解决中小物流企业融资难、发展难的后顾之忧。

最后，物流联盟应规范物流联盟合作协议，建立协调管理机制。

由于跨境物流联盟内部组织复杂，跨境电商物流联盟模式运作中级别最高的风险就是协调管理风险或称合作风险。该风险不仅不利于自身运作效率的提升，而且有可能危及跨境物流联盟的存在。要想真正规避协调管理风险，需要联盟企业建立联盟合作协调管理机制方式，规范各主体行为。该管理机制需要联盟参与的各方签订合作协议，提升合作黏性，出具物流联盟主体需履行的责任与义务详细条款，如矛盾解决方案、信息共享方式等内容，限制企业逐利行为，提升组织综合管理效能。设立联盟管理委员会提高跨境物流联盟的管理水平（田青、李桂娥，2021）。跨境电商物流联盟成员通过选择企业代表、成立合作协调管理委员会，监督各企业行为。该委员会还应根据数字化物流平台下各企业的实际分工，出台针对性协调管理机制，约束各主体的行为。另外，借助新技术如区块链的应用，可以有效解决合作中的信任问题，降低成本、提高效率。只有在合作收益大于成本的原则之下，跨境电商物流联盟才能发挥不同主体的优势，取长补短，实现跨境电商物流联盟模式的可持续发展。可持续发展的跨境电商物流联盟才能提供长期战略规划，保障模式长久、高效运作。这将是一个不断尝试、不断优化的长期过程。

第5章 海外仓的发展现状及优化——多案例研究

本章聚焦海外仓的重要性以及面临的主要问题，重点探讨海外仓的优化策略，并结合西邮物流公司（Western Post）、纵腾集团（Zongteng Group）和北京凯博锦程经贸有限公司的案例进行探讨。

5.1 海外仓简介

海外仓随跨境电商的兴起而出现。它是跨境电商企业在海外的买方国家通过租赁或建造仓库，提前将需要售出的货物通过跨境运输的方式送至海外仓库，在消费者下单后可直接从相关海外仓发货，从而将跨境的长线物流转变为"最后一公里"配送。跨境电商直邮带来的一系列问题在海外仓模式下都能够得到有效的解决。有了海外仓的头程支撑，漫长复杂的跨境物流简化为目的国的尾程物流，用户体验可得到质的提升。

根据建仓主体的不同，海外仓可以分为三种类型：第一种是大型跨境电商平台自己建设的海外仓，例如天猫、京东等跨境电商平台在海外建设的自营海外仓；第二种是物流企业建设的向跨境卖家租赁的第三方海外仓，例如顺丰、邮政等在海外建设的海外仓；第三种是政府主导建设的公共海外仓。其中，第三方海外仓占据市场的主导地位，一般是指由第三方物流企业建立并运营的海外仓库，能够为众多出口跨境电商企业提供清关、入库质检、接受订单、订单分拣、多渠道发货、后续运输等物流服务的海外仓形式。

5.2　海外仓的战略意义

2022 年的《政府工作报告》中提出，"加快发展外贸新业态新模式，充分发挥跨境电商作用，支持建设一批海外仓"。跨境电商海外仓凭借"本土化销售、去中间商、配送时效高"等特性，大大便利了国内出口企业直接面向海外终端消费者，加快了对外贸易由单纯的加工制造出口向提供全球定制化供应链服务的转变，对外贸企业充满了吸引力。海外仓功能强大，连接着跨境物流的头程运输和尾程配送，促进尾程功能提升和头程整合质变，反推电商平台的良性发展，促进国际货代的转型，从而带动传统国际贸易的产业升级。因此，海外仓不仅是跨境电商重要的境外节点，也是带动整个跨境物流生态圈整体协同发展的重要设施。作为跨境物流上的新节点，可解决跨境物流的诸多顽疾。海外仓的出现也促使跨境物流供应链转变思维，从物流思维转换为供应链思维，使跨境物流供应链整合成为可能。

5.2.1　促进尾程功能提升和头程整合质变

鲁旭（2016）论述了第三方海外仓建设对跨境供应链整合的关键作用，虽然海外仓在跨境供应链中处于中端仓储的位置，但对促进头程运输的质变整合和尾程配送的增值功能提升起着承上启下的关键作用。作为跨境物流业务的中端重要节点，海外仓除了着力开发自身的中高端增值业务，做好各方关系的协调，还能够完成顺利连接尾程配送的任务，同时做好尾程退换货的处理，帮助完成积压退货的就地销售，实现海外仓从仓储业务到销售领域的功能延伸，从整体上解决了海外仓尾程物流和逆向物流的问题，提升了尾程服务的质量。

此外，海外仓还对头程运输产生至关重要的影响。主要表现在海外仓的智能化运营能够帮助出口商准确预测市场需求，准确安排头程运输的货物选择、货物数量和目的地，及时预测补仓规模，实现头程运输的整合质变。

5.2.2 促进跨境电商平台的发展

跨境电商平台作为贸易中介，连接着制造企业和海外消费者，拥有海外仓的跨境电商平台能够提供更好的客户体验，提高产品售价，从而获得较为丰厚的利润。同时，海外仓能够集中管理出口商品，监管严格，可以避免相当大比例的跨境电商贸易纠纷，更好地维护跨境电商平台的形象，促进平台的发展。

5.2.3 促进国际货运代理的转型

据国际海运网截至 2022 年 1 月的统计数据，当前从事货运代理业务（简称货代）的企业已超过 6 万家，且同质化严重。海外仓的出现为国际货代的转型提供了良好的契机。传统国际货代可整合海运、空运、邮政和国际商业快递，形成更高效的跨境运力。同时，货代还可以向跨境仓储延伸，建设海外仓，发展海外仓的增值服务。可以说，海外仓正是国际货代转型的最佳路径。

5.3 我国海外仓的功能和发展现状

跨境电商卖家使用海外仓的一般逻辑是，根据市场需求、人口、经济水平等因素，对将来一段时间内商品的销量进行预测，预先将一定数量的货物送至海外仓，方便后续的配送环节，降低在清关、商检等流程中的时间成本，而批量规模化的运输也能够有效地降低运输过程中各个环节存在的风险，从而达到降低成本的目的（谢嘉豪，2022）。

海外仓除了有在目的国发货的功能，还有便捷处理退换货的功能。跨境电商卖家利用海外仓能够为买家提供更好、更便捷的售后服务，退换货服务更加及时。此外，海外仓也可以为退货产品提供再包装等服务，方便产品的二次销售。

当海外仓经海关批准成为保税仓库时，其功能和用途范围更为广泛，可简化海关通关流程和相关手续。同时，在保税仓库可以进行转口贸易，以海外仓所在地为第三国，连接卖方和买方国家。在保税海外仓内，还可以进行简单加工等相应增值服务，使海外仓的增值服务不仅限于退换货的二次包装，有效地丰富了仓储功能，提高了海外仓的资源利用效率。

截至 2021 年底，我国已在海外建设了 2000 多个海外仓，总占地面积超过了 1600 万平方米。① 海外仓也不断完善其功能，推动我国跨境电商与外贸不断发展。我国政策一直支持海外仓的发展，各部委、各行政部门也积极配合。商务部已经会同相关部门提出了 8 条支持海外仓发展的政策措施，包括利用外经贸发展专项资金和服务贸易创新发展引导基金等支持海外仓建设，优化海外仓监管模式备案流程。

各地海关也纷纷出台了相关的支持政策。天津海关深入贯彻落实加快发展外贸新业态新模式要求，开通海外仓业务绿色通道，简化海外仓备案手续；② 畅通热线电话、网络平台等"不跑腿""零接触"沟通渠道，为有意向开通海外仓业务的企业提供全过程"一对一"政策辅导，助力企业完成跨境电商出口的"换挡升级"，助力本土企业保订单、稳预期。③ 浙江省钱江海关推进"十地百团助千企"精准服务活动，积极助力企业推进海

---

① 商务部：海外仓数量已超 2000 个，面积超 1600 万平方米 [EB/OL]. 新浪财经，2022 - 4 - 21 [2023 - 4 - 28]. https：//baijiahao. baidu. com/s？ id = 1730704858541044415&wfr = spider&for = pc.

② 国务院政策例行吹风会 [EB/OL]. (2022 - 9 - 27) [2023 - 4 - 28]. http：//www. gov. cn/xinwen/2022zccfh/26/index. htm.

③ 天津海关推出海外仓模式破解出口物流难题助力跨境电商出口速度"换挡升级" [EB/OL]. 北方网，2022 - 11 - 20 [2023 - 4 - 28]. http：//news. enorth. com. cn/system/2022/11/20/053352730. shtml.

外仓出口业务。除此之外,商务部持续推进信息的全国联网,实现"属地备案、全国通用",支持海外仓优化市场布局,更加智慧地发挥多功能服务平台功能,继续出台支持海外仓的措施。

张赠富(2021)使用 TOPSIS 方法,选取我国 35 家比较有影响力的跨境电商企业,对其海外仓的发展现状和综合服务能力进行了测度分析。他的研究结果表明,35 家企业中有 20 家企业的测度结果高于平均值,且排名第一的跨境电商海外仓企业服务能力综合值是排名最后一名的 3.747(0.993/0.265)倍。这些数字都说明我国跨境电商海外仓服务能力差异比较明显,整体发展水平非常不平衡。

海外仓看似新热点,但其实已经发展多年,而且行业竞争激烈。如果不是 2020 年的新冠疫情,很多海外仓公司可能难以为继。疫情期间,国际供应链管控能力和运力不足,海外仓和保税仓作为跨境物流的新方式,作为备货体系的补充,很好地弥补了疫情带来的影响,不仅减轻了疫情对跨境电商卖家的海外备货影响,还能发挥本地化运营优势,以及提升物流配送时效、退换货便利等优势,这些优势使海外仓和保税仓在疫情期间也能保持较高的热度。各地政府纷纷出台支持政策,在贷款利率、贷款期限上给予优惠,支持海外仓建设。2020 年 4 月,宁波政府鼓励企业自建海外仓,自建海外仓的项目给予贷款年利率不超过 4%,贷款期限不少于两年的优惠,财政给予 50% 的贷款贴息。[1] 2023 年 1 月,天津政府落实"稳经济运行 33 条"政策,鼓励企业共建共享海外仓,加快出海步伐。对企业投资自建或租用的公共海外仓,单一国家或地区仓储面积达到 2000 平方米以上,最高给予 100 万元的资金支持。[2]

但疫情是短期刺激因素。一仓难求的繁荣在 2021 年上半年就结束了。2021 年下半年,海外仓开始降价、内卷,其经营也出现了不少新挑战。首

---

① 宁波市人民政府.《关于支持外贸企业渡难关稳订单拓市场的若干意见》政策解读 [EB/OL].(2020 - 4 - 20)[2023 - 4 - 28]. http://www.ningbo.gov.cn/art/2020/4/20/art_1229187964_53685590.html.

② 尹玉财.天津:落实稳经济 33 条政策 鼓励企业建设海外仓 [EB/OL].(2023 - 02 - 07)[2023 - 4 - 28]. http://app.myzaker.com/news/article.php?pk=63e246b98e9f0930cc51f05e.

先，国际货代转型发展海外仓时，还是延续传统货代按货值收费的经营理念，多揽货多盈利，导致很多跨境电商企业盲目跟进海外仓，大批不适合当地市场的货物被发往海外仓，导致货物积压，甚至最后因无力支付仓储费用而不得不弃货、销毁，大大影响了出口企业的海外仓体验（鲁旭，2016）。海外仓作为一种重要的跨境电商物流方式，是为了解决跨境电商企业物流成本和时效问题而出现的。然而，由于竞争激烈，海外仓企业面临着严峻的市场压力。为了降低成本，一些海外仓企业降低了服务质量，将自己定位在低端市场。这种做法可能会导致客户流失，并且难以维持企业的长期发展。

另外，虚拟海外仓的出现也是一种应对市场压力的方式。虚拟海外仓是利用互联网技术，在跨境电商平台上模拟出一个海外仓的概念，通过与国内快递公司合作，实现了发货速度快、物流成本低的理想。虽然虚拟海外仓在短时间内能够吸引客户，但其售后服务往往存在问题，如无法提供实际的海外仓存储服务以及售后服务质量不高等。此外，虚拟海外仓背负着欺骗消费者的"原罪"，一旦被曝光，将面临着严重的法律风险。

海外仓行业的发展现状表明，目前还没有形成良性协同发展的跨境物流生态系统，海外仓依然面临着严重的内卷加内耗。除海外仓经营的现实状况外，即便是成熟的海外仓企业，经营过程中仍然要面对大量的具体问题。

5.4　海外仓企业的经营困境

整体来看，目前我国跨境物流企业产品、服务同质化严重，缺乏核心竞争力。海外企业要想脱颖而出，必须构建自己的竞争壁垒，提升企业核心竞争力。海外仓的建设投入大，产出水平却与投资不符，问题主要体现在以下方面。

5.4.1　本土化水平低

本土化发展是海外仓最主要的发展趋势。目前海外仓本土化面临的主要问题一是对本土制度的认知体系须完善，尤其是当地的纳税制度。海外仓在海外大多以企业实体运营，在当地纳税是合法经营的基础。但各地税率政策差异很大，对当地税收政策的认知不足是造成税务障碍的主要原因。二是本土招聘难。海外仓使用国内员工必然涉及复杂烦琐的签证居留问题，而且本土化经营的基础就是雇用当地员工。但是在欧美等发达国家，人力成本较发展中国家来说偏高。蓝领小时工的薪资在 20 美元左右，且西方有收小费的文化，用工成本剧增。三是本土化营销困难，各目的国客户需求各异，根据客户需求提供差异化产品，同时精准确定投放数量和制定价格策略已经不易，但真正的难点是在跨文化基础上的精准营销，各国文化、习惯等方面存在巨大差异，做针对性的营销和平台引流都有很大的挑战（谢桂梅，2022）。

5.4.2　客户满意度低

目前跨境电商物流费用在整个跨境电商成本中的占比为 20%～30%，跨境物流投入大，客户满意度却很难提升。根据"3C"数码电子产品跨境电商平台（FocalPrice）的客户满意度调查，客户对跨境电商的抱怨集中在物流方面。即便是国内首屈一指的跨境电商平台设立的海外仓，也很难收获较高的客户满意度。① 熊俊、朱思怡（2021）以"凯博锦程"为例研究了海外仓主要的物流问题分布，发现退换货问题造成的客户不满意占到51%。因此，对退换货处理不及时是造成客户满意度不高的主要原因。当

---

① 先略研究院. 目前跨境电商物流费用在整个跨境电商成本中占到了 20%～30%［EB/OL］.（2022 - 09 - 14）［2023 - 04 - 28］. https：//business. sohu. com/a/584830766_121333014；文汇客户端. 物流成本在跨境电商卖家支出中占到四分之一，怎么破？［OL］. 2019 - 10 - 21［20223 - 4 - 28］. https：//wenhui. whb. cn/third/baidu/201910/21/295936. html.

买家收到货物选择退换货物之后，由于公司处理单据的速度缓慢，退换货平均处理时长为 2 周，这就导致了退换货的时效性较低，因此消费者满意度低，整体体验较差。另外，对客户需求把握不准，企业面对不同国家和地区的客户，语言、文化、风俗、消费习惯等差异很大，而海外仓企业员工的跨文化意识和跨文化能力普遍不强，因此，海外仓企业对当地客户需求很难精准把握，导致后续的产品研发、设计、营销和配送等环节很难精准匹配客户需求，无法为消费者提供满意的线上购物体验。

5.4.3　物流生态协同度低

根据跨境物流供应链生态系统所示，海外仓企业除了要确保供应链的顺畅运行，还需要在支付、通关、缴税、金融和法律法规等方面做好生态系统构建的综合协同服务，这直接影响着交货速度、资金安全、通关效率以及合规纳税等环节。我国海外仓企业的生态系统功能协同还面临诸多困难。例如，跨境物流面临的困难之一就是清关效率低。海外仓业务的特点就是订单数量大，频次高但是单价低，每一单都需要一一完成通关、商检、监管等环节，流程烦琐频次高。而跨境电商又要求较高的通关效率，这样的矛盾会大大增加清关流程的不确定性，清关遇阻的概率较大。海外仓在目的国清关过程中，也面临着各国海关管理规则存在差异、清关手续繁杂的问题。跨境电商商品品类多、通关频次多也会增加商检的难度，造成商检效率低。且目前申报和办理清关程序通常是由电商企业自主完成的，没有专业清关公司的帮助，清关不确定性较多。

5.4.4　物流集成度低

海外仓连接了头程运输和目的国物流，各个物流阶段的集成和衔接直接影响了海外仓的运作和成本。目前跨境物流集成度较低，主要表现在三个方面：一是头程运输成本高。头程运输一般来说是指使用"铁＋空＋海"等运输方式或者运输方式的组合，将商家的货物通过大宗商品的运输模式运输到目的国的海外仓。头程运输包括了境内运输、海上运输及目的国运输等环节，跨境运输涉及通关、商检等流程，且各国海关的通关流程不同，手续复杂。因此，由电商企业自行安排头程运输，必然会造成头程物流成本高、风险大的问题。二是海外仓运营成本高。自建海外仓的前期投入巨大，运营成本高，只适合实力雄厚的电商企业。对于大多数电商企业而言，租赁海外仓是更好的选择。海外仓的运营成本较高，主要集中在人工、能耗以及租赁费用上。且海外仓重复建设严重，对现有已建仓的利用率低，资源浪费严重。三是海外仓增值服务整体水平低。目前，海外仓的增值服务局限于分拣、包装等，增值水平低，且不完全覆盖商家最关心的退换货以及维修等服务，导致卖家不得不将商品退回商品原产地进行更换或维修，这也意味着卖家成本的增加。

5.4.5 数字化水平低

跨境电商业务量不断增长，但是海外仓的数字化水平却没有相应的提升，严重限制了跨境电商业务的发展。海外仓发展初期，业务量较小，海外仓运作的模式通常是在海外当地预定好仓库，甚至是一个简单的车库用于存放货物，接到订单后安排发货即可，操作流程很简单。但这种作坊式的运作方式仅适用于存货量和订单量都相对较少的状态。一旦订单量激增，就必然出现发错货、库存不准、终端配送贵、无法兼顾逆向物流的情况，进而难以提供满意的售后服务，派送车辆无法保证，无法按照仓库地址实现智能分仓发货等，造成海外仓配送失序。目前海外仓运行系统需要保证比较高的信息化水平，以保证对各个环节的快速响应（王立鹤等，2022）。"凯博锦程"目前使用的是企业资源计划（ERP）系统管理，这也是目前海外仓公司采用的主流系统。该系统利用人工进行复核，未使用大数据，造成物流信息跟踪时效性差，易出现错发漏发的现象。因此，对仓储配送进行规范化和数字化管理，实施仓储管理系统（WMS）、扫码枪、出入库管理、拣货路径设置等措施势在必行。张赠富（2021）设计了海外仓综合服务能力的测度指标体系，权重最大的分别是交易额和自动化程度，这表明海外仓的规模以及其信息化服务能力决定了海外仓的综合服务能力。

综上所述,海外仓前期建设阶段需要在短时间投入较大的资金量,由于海外仓建设在不同地点,难以形成规模效益以降低成本,需要雄厚的资金支持,建设周期长、回报见效慢,中小企业难以承受(葛岩,2016)。若海外仓本土化水平不高,制度政策和文化距离问题凸显,海外仓无法融入本地经营,导致无论是在物流管理上还是本土化营销上都无法实现既定的目标,这也是目前海外仓服务无法获得较高的客户满意度的原因。即便是实力雄厚的企业建成了海外仓,依靠企业自身的资源也很难在短时间内解决运营问题。我国参与跨境电商经营的中小型企业较多,结合我国国情,由政府牵头建设公共海外仓更适合中国跨境电商的发展。

5.5 海外仓运作模式的优化

海外仓的建设和运营不仅需要大量的资金投入,还需要对目标市场的文化、政策、法规、行业标准等方面进行了解和适应,同时也需要具备全球物流运营和管理的能力。因此,海外仓的建设面临宏观和微观的双重风险和考验。随着跨境电商渗透率的加速和提升,未来我国跨境市场潜力依然巨大,前景依然乐观。竞争和内卷只是暂时的,跨境物流行业的机遇大于挑战。截至 2021 年 12 月,我国海外仓数量已超过 2000 个,总面积超过 1600 万平方米,积累了一定的经验和基础。其中,在北美洲、欧洲、亚洲等地区的海外仓总数量占比接近海外仓建设总量的 90%。以上这些数据都充分表明,海外仓发展的大趋势不会改变,但运作模式还有待进一步优化。

从宏观来看,仅靠跨境物流第三方企业自发建设,很难保证海外仓战略的实现,还需要政府的扶持。2022 年 12 月国务院印发的《"十四五"现代物流发展规划》中提出,应加快布局企业海外仓的落地,加快境外物流网络服务能力的稳步提升。鲁旭(2016)指出,国家助力海外仓发展,除了在融资方面给予一些优惠政策，还要引导和鼓励与海外仓相关的服务业"走出去"，如保险、法律、财务、咨询、信息等，共同助力打造以第三方物流公司为主的跨境物流供应链。跨境物流企业可充分利用国家对海外仓的发展扶持政策，勇于开拓新的海外仓发展区域，在海外仓选址上避免扎堆，选择政治环境良好且具有贸易往来前景的区域建仓，如"两沿十廊"国际物流大通道沿线国家，对接"区域全面经济伙伴关系协定"（RCEP）的区域国家等。[①] 杨洁（2022）提出，在我国跨境贸易的重点区域，可通过大型物流企业联合设立基金等多种形式筹建海外仓，为难以实现自建海外仓的中小企业提供必要的仓储和配套服务。随着海外仓业务的发展，一些类似"虚拟海外仓"的业务悄然出现，对这样的新生事物要进行严格规范，更好地对接跨境物流的海外规则，在规则允许的范围内实现良性发展。因此，随着海外仓的发展，也要加强对海外仓创新演变的规范化管理，进一步规范海外仓服务标准，从顶层设计层面制定跨境电商海外仓标准、海外仓运营规范等，提升海外仓企业合规化水平，为企业建设运营海外仓提供专业化指导。

以上是宏观层面的跨境电商制度环境建设，包括制定跨境电商政策，加强跨境电商监管，推动标准化，促进国际合作，除此之外，还应加强知识产权保护，加强体系的抗风险能力，并大力培养跨境电商人才。跨境电商的制度环境可以促进跨境电商的健康发展，提高跨境电商的市场化程度，降低跨境电商的交易风险和成本，增加跨境电商的国际竞争力。

微观来看，海外仓企业须大力提高物流生态协同水平，要与物流企业、仓储企业、海关、商检、税收、支付平台等构成的生态系统进行有效协同；提升本土化的经营水平，深入目的国，在整体提升跨文化经营水平上，利用信息化技术实现精准本土化营销；提高物流集成水平，实现质量管理、营销推广、渠道建设、物流运输、仓储配送、报关报检、支付结算、售后服务等各种服务的集成和整合。在整个跨境电商生态系统中，海

---

① 现代物流领域首份国家级五年规划提出：构建国际国内物流大通道［N/OL］. 人民日报，（2023 – 01 – 03）［2023 – 04 – 28］. http：//www. gov. cn/xinwen/2023 – 01 – 03/content_5734669. htm.

外仓虽是最后一站，却是整个物流供应链生态系统中的核心模块，对组织构建智慧、稳定、高效的全链路跨境物流生态系统至关重要。下面在物流生态圈建设的基础上，从物流生态协同能力、本土化经营能力、物流集成能力、智能运营能力和客户服务提升能力五个方面论述海外仓经营模式的优化。

5.5.1　物流生态协同能力

跨境物流生态系统的各个环节相互协作才能实现整个生态系统的正常高效率运转。为实现生态系统内各个链条的便捷高效运行，支付结算、通关税收和金融等环节的协同运转共同提升至关重要。这也关系着资金安全以及通关效率，物流速度、合规纳税等各环节的顺利运行，从而影响整个生态圈的运作。物流生态协同性的研究，除了供应链各个链条的协同（杜志平，2018，2020；张夏恒，2016；张夏恒、张荣刚，2018），还包括一些更为细化的研究，主要集中在高效清关和合规运营方面（熊俊，2021；王立鹤等，2022）。在清关效率方面，积极提升通关效率，加强与国际机构及政府部门的沟通，推动各国在海关监管方面进一步对接国际规则。此外，跨境电商企业也要从自身出发，积极寻求更便捷的通关方式，如建立自己的清关公司，以更专业和专注的方式操作通关业务。早在 2016 年，作为中国全境至欧美中大件全物流链条的综合性服务提供者，西邮物流就在美国、英国、德国、比利时设立了 4 个独立的清关子公司。纵腾集团 2022 年也重点推动"端到端海外履约供应链服务"①，其中就包括海外国际卡车运输干线，提供海外清关和海外分拨等专业化服务。②

---

① 福建纵腾网络有限公司（简称"纵腾集团"）成立于 2009 年，以"全球跨境电商基础设施服务商"为企业定位，聚焦跨境仓储与物流，提供海外仓储、商业专线物流、定制化物流等一体化物流解决方案，旗下拥有谷仓海外仓、云途物流、WORLDTECH 等知名品牌。

② 纵腾集团副总裁李聪：全球端到端供应链渐成潮流［J/OL］. 亿邦动力. 2022 - 07 - 29 ［2023 - 4 - 28］. https：//baijiahao. baidu. com/s? id = 1739688458425636340&wfr = spider&for = pc.

物流生态协同的另外一个环节就是合规纳税，前提是了解目的国税收政策并建立与当地税收管理部门的沟通和联动，构建海外仓在目的国合法经营的生态系统。跨境电商企业在海外仓运营中，应明确海外仓主体位置，积极了解目的国的税收政策，依法纳税。熊俊、朱思怡（2021）指出，为提升纳税效率，跨境电商企业要协调推动税收监管方式的电子化，适应电商新业态发展。在国际合作中，积极推动相关机构和政府之间的税务合作，实现税收程序电子化、凭证互认，避免重复征税。

5.5.2　本土化经营能力

肖亮等（2019）指出，本土化能力是跨境电商企业综合实力的重要表现，主要包括本土化物流服务能力、本土化分销服务能力以及本土化冲突协调能力这三个维度。这三个维度分别反映了企业在目的国市场不同方面的本土化水平。首先，本土化物流服务能力是指企业在目的国能够迅速响应市场物流服务需求，提供高效仓储配送服务和退换货服务的能力。其次，本土化分销服务能力则强调企业在目的国利用和整合分销资源，提供高效的产品销售，包括品牌推广、产品销售、渠道服务和展示体验等。最后，本土化冲突协调能力则要求企业能够运用目的国的关系资源，协调解决各类冲突和纠纷，确保企业在目的国市场的顺利运营。总之，跨境电商企业需要在这三个方面不断提升本土化能力，以适应目的国市场的需求，实现跨境电商的可持续发展。

对跨境电商企业来说，本土化的经营能力是个多层次、多侧面的综合能力，既包括在本土建仓的能力，也包括建仓成功后的本土化经营能力。首先，在建立海外仓时就应组建本土化的经营管理团体，加大对本土人才的雇用力度。毕竟每个国家的文化和政策等都有所不同，国人对本国的思想文化相对熟悉，对目的国家地区的文化比较陌生，而且思想观念等都难以在短时间内转换，组建本土化团队才能真正实现本土化经营。其次，应注重向消费者提供本土化综合服务，以本土化语言为沟通方式，提供本土化支付方式和基于海外仓的本土化发货。这就要求跨境电商企业充分考察、了解本土习俗、法律法规和当地消费者偏好，精准营销。在本土化支付方面，必须谨慎选择合适的第三方支付平台，提供本土化支付接口，实现本土化支付。在本土化发货方面，应在目标国本地仓库储存足够数量的商品，从本地仓及时发货，减少物流环节，提高效益。西邮公司是本土化经营成功的范例，该公司的全球自营仓库数量超过 25 个。这些自营仓分布在美国、德国、英国等，涵盖了欧美主流国家，形成了"洛杉矶仓储群""新泽西仓储群""休斯敦仓储群""芝加哥仓储群""亚特兰大仓储群"等本土化经营典型公司集群。[①]

5.5.3　物流集成能力

海外仓的功能绝不仅限于单一的仓储，它与前端的海运干线、空运干线紧密相连，与后端的 B2B 大货配送、B2C 包裹配送密不可分。将前后端进行一体化整合是海外仓实现成本降低和效率提高的必然趋势。企业可以通过海运的方式实现低成本运输，然后将商品存储在海外仓内，进行统一管理并提供增值服务，如简单分装和再包装等。当客户下单后，可以通过本地化的物流配送系统快速交货，提高交货速度，提高客户体验和满意度。因此，本土化交货是海外仓的重要优势之一，而功能的整合将进一步提高海外仓的优势。

海外仓的集成运作就是不断提高物流资源整合能力，提高跨境物流的协同度，在分析本企业的产品特点、业务覆盖区域和运输需求特点基础上，寻求与专业化的海运、铁路、汽运等第三方物流公司及本地化的物流企业合作，解决头程及尾程运输的细节问题。在头程运输中，根据目的国位置及运输货物特点灵活组合不同的运输方式。在尾程运输中，与当地物流企业合作，及时快捷地完成尾程配送。西邮公司就是积极探索本地化物流能力建设，不断提高本土化量身定制的服务能力的成功案例。西邮公司

---

① 西邮物流. 祝贺大件海外仓西邮物流荣获 2022 晓生排行榜海外仓十强企业［EB/OL］. (2022 - 06 - 07)［2023 - 4 - 28］. https：//baijiahao. baidu. com/s? id = 1734968436357734093&wfr = spider&for = pc.

自建卡车团队完成本地物流任务。在去港口提货时，自营卡车团队更加方便调度。这种优势，在新冠疫情期间卡车司机严重短缺的情况下，体现得更为明显。同时，在终端配送时，西邮自营的卡车团队，能降低配送成本。类似的自营运输网络建设者还有很多，一些海外仓龙头企业也开始在提高海运和空运运力方面布局。如纵腾集团首架波音宽体货机 B777F 首航沙特阿拉伯利雅得机场①，这波操作让纵腾掌握了一定的自持运力，提高了其供应链服务的稳定性。

鼓励海外仓企业针对特定细分品类和特定客群等打造大件仓、SKD仓、定制仓和退货中转仓等专业型海外仓。例如，西邮公司多年专注于打造大件仓的运营模式，在创立初期就专注于跨境物流行业的"大件产品的行业解决方案"②，且专注服务中大型品牌客户。这种竞争策略让西邮公司轻松度过波动的行业周期。专注大件，意味着要放弃占比较高的小件产品；专注中大型品牌客户，意味着要放弃很多小型卖家，但正是这种聚焦，让他们用短短几年时间树立了竞争壁垒，即"大件产品的行业解决方案"。另外，纵腾集团的"纵腾—谷仓海外仓"也已发展十余年，重点发展大件家具和汽配等大件类目，实现海外仓服务专业化发展。

提高海外仓高端增值服务能力，即海外仓充分利用本土经营的优势发展增值业务。例如，将海外仓的进仓操作延伸至海关接货，可以大大减少出口企业货物过关的后顾之忧。同理，仓储管理中也可以增加包装管理等基础的增值业务。鲁旭（2016）提出，在货物进仓后，海外仓可以与保险公司合作，将物流服务延伸至运输保险和仓储保险领域。此外，海外仓还将担负起税收载体的任务，帮助跨境电商企业完成规范的目的国纳税。总之，海外仓作为海外经营的实体以及出口商在目的国的代理，需完成各方关系协调的重要任务。

---

① 纵腾集团首架波音宽体货机完成首航［N/OL］. 电商报.（2022 – 10 – 08）［2023 – 04 – 28］. https：//www. dsb. cn/news – flash/102896. html.

② Windowsfang. 深度：我们需要怎样的海外仓？［EB/OL］.（2022 – 04 – 30）［2023 – 4 – 28］. https：//baijiahao. baidu. com/s?id =1731500414120735655&wfr = spider&for = pc.

5.5.4　智能运营能力

相对于传统海外仓库，现代海外仓最大的特点在于数字化水平的提升，可以实现智慧运营、智能布货、智能可视化系统等，通过数字化、智能化系统，深度挖掘数据，分析客户需求、消费偏好，并根据行业热度、供应能力、库存调配等信息，调整产品配比、营销方式和服务策略，完善智慧生态系统。王立鹤等（2022）将智能化生态系统总结为如下环节：供应链整体设计、流程管理、营销选品、需求预测、可视物流、智慧金融、智慧采购、智慧仓储、智慧配送、智慧售后，这些环节共同构成了网络化、智能化生态系统。

西邮公司通过智慧物流的布局，提升其智慧化运营能力。在大促期间，很多海外仓无法预约到 FedEx 车辆，导致大量订单信息无法及时上网，影响客户店铺指标。西邮通过智能计算，提前把库存下沉到各个仓库，分摊单一仓储的配送流量，完美地解决了大促期间的 FedEx 车辆短缺问题。同时，西邮公司还提前布局智能可视化系统，客户可以清晰地看到每个仓的发货数据，进而辅助配货决策。在货物从工厂运到海外仓库的运输过程中，西邮打造了 30 个可视化节点，客户可以随时查看运输状态。西邮的运营离不开智能化的数据系统，他们投入了大量的 IT 人员，自行研发了数智大脑、运营中台、协同平台、运输系统、仓储系统、中转系统等。也就是说，从头程的运输，到港仓转运，再到入仓、分拣、出仓，以及末端配送，西邮有一整套系统连接节点，并可以提供清晰准确的相关数据。

5.5.5　客户服务提升能力

海外仓集成化和智能化经营的实现，并不意味着其客户体验的必然升级。作为属地经营的主体，海外仓还须切实提升自身的客户服务能力。为了避免行业同质化带来的激烈竞争，参照本地营销模式，对标本土竞争对手，不断增加客户黏性，提升客户忠诚度，提高在目的国市场的竞争力。

一是海外仓经营应着力提升客户满意度。海外仓企业的发展理念要以客户需求为中心，站在目的国文化和价值观立场，深入研究本土客户的需求特点、消费心理、购买习惯，收集数据进行深度分析，制定出相匹配的营销服务策略，提高客户体验感。二是服务的定位要确保精准。海外仓企业除服务消费者之外，也要服务中小型企业客户，海外仓储和配送能力也应有一个清晰准确的定位，努力为客户提供定制化配送服务。不同行业对仓储物流的要求会相差很大，例如一些客单价高的 3C 电子产品，需要服务商支持"唯一码管理"（每个商品都有一个单独的码），以便处理售后问题。如果没有这项服务，一旦遇到用次品恶意投诉并要求退货的买家，卖家将难以申诉。目前，西邮在家居、家电、3C 电子行业形成了成熟的解决方案。不管是家具产品、家电产品的逆向物流，还是高端 3C 电子产品的"唯一码管理"，他们都有完整的专业解决方案。①

---

① Windowsfang. 深度：我们需要怎样的海外仓？［EB/OL］.（2022 - 04 - 30）［2023 - 04 - 28］. https：//baijiahao. baidu. com/s?id = 1731500414120735655&wfr = spider&for = pc.

Chapter 1　Cross-border E-commerce and Logistics and Supply Chain Ecosystem

This chapter focuses on Cross-border E-commerce, its ecosystem, and the associated logistics and supply chain systems, and further examines their integration and collaboration.

1.1　Cross-border E-commerce

1.1.1　Definition of Cross-border E-commerce

Cross-border E-commerce can be classified in both a broad sense and a narrow sense. In a broad sense, Cross-border E-commerce refers to all commercial activities conducted through electronic means, including data transmission, contract negotiation and signing, bill transmission, Cross-border finance, Cross-border logistics and other activities. In a narrow sense, Cross-border E-commerce refers to platform-based Cross-border E-commerce commercial activities. It includes Cross-border B2B, B2C and C2C models, mostly the B2C model. The flows of goods, logistics, capital and information constitute the four dimensions of Cross-border E-commerce. According to *Baidu Encyclopedia*, Cross-border E-commerce refers to the E-commerce platform or online trading platform where trading entities belonging to different customs areas reach transactions agreements, conduct payment and settlement through E-commerce platforms, deliver goods and finally complete transactions through Cross-border logistics. Defined from the perspective of transaction process, it is a narrow-sense definition, which is also the research object of this book. It is a network and electronic-based development of traditional international trade. Thanks to the Internet, information and communication technology and modern logistics, with international business as the core, Cross-border E-commerce changed the traditional selling and shopping channels by breaking the tangible and intangible boundaries among regions and countries, reducing the physical face-to-face onsite communication, saving traditional transaction costs. Thus, it gains popularity around the world. It has become a new form of global international trade and a new driving force for China's economic growth.

A traditional Cross-border trade process goes like this: domestic manufacturing enterprises—domestic exporters—foreign importers—wholesalers—retailers—consumers. Products go through multiple middlemen from manufacturing enterprises to consumers, and the channel cost is high. The development of Cross-border E-commerce has greatly diminished intermediate links, thus reducing costs spent on various channels. When domestic enterprises connect directly with foreign retailers and even end-users (consumers), the direct export chain reduces costs that are spent on various marketing channels and improves the efficiency of the supply chain. China's Cross-border E-commerce import and export sales has increased nearly 10 times in the past five years since 2017. The percentage of Cross-border E-commerce in foreign trade has increased from less than 1% in 2015 to 4.9% in 2021. Cross-border E-commerce has become a new growth point of China's economy.

Cross-border E-commerce has effectively promoted the integration of global economy and the globalization of trade, not only breaking the physical boundaries of countries, making international trade borderless, but also bringing great changes in the structure and mode of world economy and trade. For individuals, enterprises, industries, countries and the world economic structure, an open, multi-dimensional and three-dimensional multilateral economic and trade cooperation model built by Cross-border E-commerce has greatly broadened channels for producers and consumers to enter the international market. It is conducive to the development of logistics and supply chain around the world, improves the optimal allocation of resources around the world, and enables enterprises to achieve mutual benefits and win-win results. Consumers can easily obtain commodity information and buy high-quality but cheap goods. Enterprises can access more customer groups. Consumers from all over the world have a larger market of products and better service experience. For a country, the production and manufacturing capacity can be fulfilled, and the effect of scale economics can be realized in a better way. The industrial chain can extend to the world, drive the development of relevant industries (such as manufacturing, logistics, payment, information technology, big data, cloud computing, blockchain) and industrial alliance, improve the industrial production and manufacturing capacity of a country, and promote the economic development of both parties. It brings more benefits to the world.

1. 1. 2   Participants of Cross-border E-commerce

From the micro perspective, Cross-border E-commerce is a complex network system and also a complex industrial ecosystem. There are many participants in both importing and exporting. The core participants are different Cross-border E-commerce e-retailing platforms. Other participants include producers, manufacturers, consumers, payment platform enterprises (i. e. financial institutions, including commercial banks, foreign exchange institutions, third-party payment enterprises), Cross-border logistics providers (and platforms) (including freight forwarders, third-party logistics, fourth-party logistics, Cross-border logistics alliances), government departments (such as customs, commodity inspection bureaus) , in- dustry societies and associations, technical support enterprises (such as Tele-com- munication service institutions, information technology institutions, network plat- form construction enterprises) , and Cross-border marketing enterprises, as shown in Figure 1 – 1.

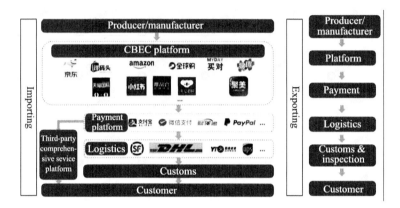

Figure 1 – 1   Participants of Cross-border E-commerce (micro-level)

From the macro perspective, Cross-border E-commerce, which runs mainly around the Cross-border transaction of goods and services, belongs to the scope of international trade. It involves the economic and trade rules, political relations among countries, the economic development level of trading parties, social cul- ture, customs and habits of trading countries, and more importantly, it is subject to international regulations (such as intellectual property agreements, privacy protec- tion, data transmission agreements, etc.) or regional organization rules. All partici- pants interact with each other and jointly maintain the sound development of Cross-border E-commerce ecosystem. Each participant of Cross-border E-com- merce is linked like a chain. Any change of one participant would possibly affect the relevant links, and might gradually be amplified along the chain, thus affecting the operation of the entire Cross-border E-commerce.

1. 2   Cross-border E-commerce Ecosystem

As mentioned earlier, Cross-border E-commerce takes the Cross-border E-commerce platform as the core and has a wide range of participants, forming a Cross-border E-commerce ecosystem. Many scholars have defined and studied the Cross-border E-commerce ecosystem from different perspectives considering different priorities. The construction of the ecosystem has gone through a process from one dimension to three dimensions. The composition of the ecosystem has gone from the initial three-player ecosystem (core player—supportive player—technical service player) to the four-species ecosystem (core species—critical species—supportive species—external environment) , to the current five-level structure (core species—critical species—supportive species—peripheral species—external environment). The structure and function of the Cross-border E-commerce ecosystem are gradually refined.

1. 2. 1   Literature Review

Zhang Wei (2016), based on the perspective of platform strategy, used the platform business model theory to layout China's transnational E-commerce ecosystem, as shown in Figure 1 – 2. She emphasized the important role of network and information technology in the Cross-border E-commerce ecosystem and believed that the Cross-border E-commerce ecosystem consists of core layer, supportive layer and technical service layer. The core layer is composed of the platform and the buyers and sellers on the platform. The supportive layer is composed of logistics service providers, financial service providers, Internet service providers and their corresponding information service platforms. The technical service layer provides various big data services, cloud computing services, and it is mainly completed by platform operation service providers, software service providers, and marketing service providers, etc. The transmission of information and data in the whole system is seamlessly connected to maintain the operation of the whole system. This ecosystem is in line with the needs of the development and competition of foreign trade enterprises in the "Internet plus" era. The study concluded that building a Cross-border E-commerce ecosystem using platform theory can achieve information sharing, strengthen the links between relevant enterprises, improve work efficiency, and ultimately achieve the coordinated development of the entire ecosystem.

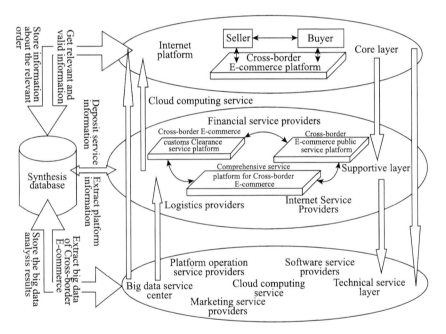

Figure 1 – 2   Cross-border E-commerce Ecosystem (Zhang Wei, 2016)

Xiong Li and Ye Kaiwen (2020) held the opinion that the Cross-border E-commerce ecosystem included three layers: the core layer was the active community, including suppliers, consumers and Cross-border E-commerce platforms, which was formed in the exploration and development period before 2007. With

the development of the industry, the supportive layer around the core layer developed, including the supportive community which provided public services and implemented supervision and the service community which provided customs declaration, logistics, payment and other services. The supportive community is relatively
special, which restricted the service community, regulated the activity community,
and participated in the formulation and implementation of Cross-border E-commerce policies. The outermost layer was the macro factors, namely, the environmental layer, including the economic, social and technological context. The
process of policy formulation was also the evolution process of Cross-border
E-commerce ecosystem.

Zhang Xiaheng and Guo Hailing(2016) introduced the concept of species to
explore the Cross-border logistics and supply chain ecosystem. They believed that
the Cross-border E-commerce ecosystem consisted of five species: core species,
critical species, supportive species, parasitic species and environment, as shown in
Figure 1 – 3. The core species was Cross-border E-commerce platform, which was
also an important node of information flow. Consumers and producers who had access to the platform were considered to be critical species. Logistics enterprises
and Cross-border payment enterprises who were closely related to logistics and
capital flow were supportive species, while Cross-border marketing and advertising, consulting institutions, and technical support enterprises were parasitic species. The internal environment and social external environment of enterprises constitute environmental factors (species). The five species cooperated with each
other to complete the operation of goods flow. On this basis, the coordination of
various species in the ecosystem, especially the coordination of Cross-border
E-commerce and Cross-border logistics and supply chain, was the top priority.

Cao Wujun *et al.* (2019) drew on the above Cross-border E-commerce ecosystem framework, emphasized its integrity and systematism, and introduced an
integrative thinking pattern. It was believed that the Cross-border E-commerce
ecosystem was a whole organic unit composed of relevant species to complete
commodity transaction with the Cross-border E-commerce platform as the core

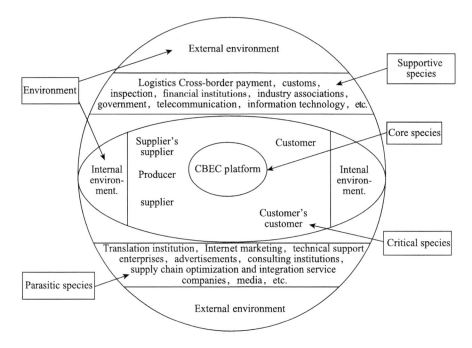

Figure 1 – 3 Ecosystem of CBEC(Zhang Xiaheng,2016;Cao Wujun *et al.* ,2019)

component under the Internet conditions. Individuals, enterprises, organizations or institutions related to Cross-border E-commerce activities constituted the species of the system. The Cross-border E-commerce platform was the medium and channel for communication and transmission. Each species formed its own fixed position. They complemented with each other's advantages and shared resources through various forms to realize the dynamic flow, communication, sharing and circulation of goods, capital, logistics and information between species and the environment.

These ecosystem theories emphasize the core role of Cross-border E-commerce platforms. A lot of studies have reached a consensus on this point. However, on the status of Cross-border logistics, there are different views. For example, Zhang Xiaheng (2016) believed that Cross-border logistics was a supportive species. In practical business operations, Cross-border logistics and Cross-border E-commerce were so closely related. As a key element in the development of

Cross-border E-commerce, Cross-border logistics is closely related to Cross-border E-commerce. The business of Cross-border logistics depends on the development of Cross-border E-commerce industry, and the development of Cross-border E-commerce is based on an efficient logistics system. An efficient Cross-border logistics and supply chain is the basis and guarantee for the development of Cross-border E-commerce. The coordinative development of the two can not only promote the development of the two industries but also enable the integration of the two industries to achieve better result. Both the industry and academia shared the view on the coordinated development of Cross-border E-commerce and logistics and supply chain (Fu Shuaishuai et al. ,2021; Zhang Xiaheng,2016; Zhang Xiaheng, Guo Hailing,2016; Wang Yunan,2022; Mi Yan,2022; Lin Ziqing,2020; Du Zhiping, Ou Yuxian, 2020; Han Lingbing et al. ,2018; Yang Zi et al. ,2018; Qi Fei,2020) ,and had carried out extensive research and put forward a number of suggestions and countermeasures.

In practice, it shows that, especially since the pandemic in 2020, Cross-border logistics has experienced sharp fluctuations of supply chain rupture and recovery. For example, in 2022, the unit price of a 20TEU container from China to the western part of the United States dropped sharply, from the highest quotation of 20,000 dollars/container during the pandemic to less than 2,000 dollars[1], and the price was less than 1/10 of the peak price in 2020, bringing huge losses to Cross-border logistics transportation enterprises and Cross-border enterprises. The macro-level considerations of global economic recession, geopolitics, carbon peak and carbon neutrality, etc. have led to increased tariffs and more complex rules. The Sino-US trade friction, consumer psychology in the post-pandemic era, changes in international trade rules, the prevalence of regional economic agreement, concerns on data collection and transmission, personal privacy, and consideration of labor and moral issues have greatly changed the external environment for the

---

[1] https://business. sohu. com/a/592481307_121123842,18 – 1 – 2023.

development of Cross-border E-commerce. The external environment is becoming increasingly important in the development of Cross-border E-commerce. As the key supporting force of Cross-border E-commerce, the development of Cross-border logistics is also increasingly subject to changes in the international environment. Therefore, in the Cross-border E-commerce ecosystem, PESTEL factors have become increasingly important determinants.

1. 2. 2   Cross-border E-commerce Ecosystem Based on PESTEL Theory

Based on the importance of external environmental factors in reality, this chapter uses PESTEL theory to analyze Cross-border E-commerce and logistics and supply chain. PESTEL analysis, known as macro-environment analysis, is an effective tool for macro-environment analysis. It can not only analyze the external environment but also identify all factors that have an impact on a result. The model entails six major environmental factors: political, economic, social, technological, environmental and legal. According to previous studies, most scholars believe that information systems, the Internet and other technical elements are closely related to Cross-border E-commerce and logistics and constitute the technical basis of Cross-border E-commerce ecology. The technological factor is more of a general trend of technology advancement than some specific innovation and application of an individual company. Therefore, the macro environment of Cross-border E-commerce is composed of six factors: PESTEL.

From the micro-level perspective, on the one hand, the Cross-border E-commerce and Cross-border logistics are not so coordinatively developed, which has become the "pain point" of Cross-border E-commerce. On the other hand, the Cross-border E-commerce ecosystem must consider more external environmental factors to better promote the long-term and stable development of Cross-border E-commerce on the micro-level. Therefore, from the perspective of long-term, sustainable and benign development of Cross-border E-commerce and its logistics and supply chain, this book constructs a Cross-border E-commerce ecosystem, as shown in Figure 1 – 4, and analyzes the Cross-border E-commerce logistics and supply chain ecosystem, as well as its development, challenges, management and optimization.

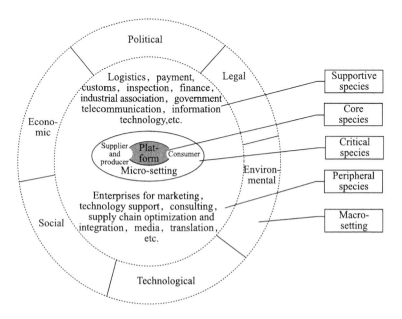

Figure 1 – 4   Cross-border E-commerce Ecosystem Supported by PESTEL Theory

1. 2. 2. 1   Micro-setting Species

(1) Core Species

Cross-border E-commerce platform is an original and great application of modern information technology and is the core species in the Cross-border E-commerce ecosystem. It is the origin of the entire Cross-border E-commerce ecosystem and the chief resource allocator and initiator in the ecosystem. Through the commodity trading platform, the system provides goods information, collects transaction information, supervises the transaction process, offers payment assistant, provides after-sales and other financing services, and plays the role of resource integration and coordination of the entire Cross-border E-commerce ecosystem.

(2) Critical Species

The direct transaction subjects of Cross-border E-commerce transactions constitute the critical species: buyers and sellers of Cross-border commodity transactions. The sellers can be extended to suppliers, manufacturers, investors and suppliers of the suppliers, and the buyers can be extended to customers and customers' customers. These species receive service of other species in the whole ecosystem. For Cross-border logistics, it is also the direct service object of the logistics and supply chain.

(3) Supportive Species

Supportive species is the species that has the closest relationship with Cross-border E-commerce, specifically referring to the relevant enterprises, departments or institutions that support Cross-border E-commerce transactions, including Cross-border payment enterprises, Cross-border logistics enterprises, customs, commodity inspection departments, financial institutions, industry associations, relevant government departments, Tele-communication and technical support organizations, etc. supportive species, as the name implies, is also the species that carries out supporting activities around the core and critical species and supports the lowest level of normal operation of Cross-border E-commerce ecosystem. As a key supportive species, Cross-border logistics and supply chain is the research topic of this book and also the "pain point" of the whole Cross-border E-commerce.

(4) Peripheral Species

Peripheral species, also known as parasitic species in previous studies (Zhang Xiaheng 2016, Cao Wujun et al. ,2019) , is the species of service provider who provides value-added services for Cross-border E-commerce transactions, including Cross-border online marketing service providers, various technology outsourcing service providers, E-commerce consulting service providers, supply chain optimization and integration service providers, and other logistics value-added service providers (such as supply chain companies and Cross-border logistics alliances). We think the word *parasite* has negative connotation and thus name the factor as peripherical species in an objective way after considering the relationship of the species with the core species.

The above four species make up the micro-ecological environment of Cross-border E-commerce.

1. 2. 2. 2   Macro-setting Factors

Macro-setting factors are the external environment of Cross-border E-commerce which includes political environment (such as political system, political relations among countries, etc.), economic environment (such as economic system and economic development level of countries, etc.), social environment (such as culture, religion, population composition, age, moral standards, labor protection, etc.), technological environment (such as Internet infrastructure, mobile network and mobile equipment penetration rate, etc.), environmental protection (such as carbon emission requirements, health and safety standards, etc.) and regulatory environment (such as tariff, quantity, quality, category and other requirements and standards of the importing country, etc.). The external environment is the basis and guarantee for the long-term and stable development of Cross-border E-commerce, which is embodied in the current wave of anti-globalization, the recession of the world economy, inflation and Sino-US trade conflicts, etc.

The micro-and macro-setting of Cross-border E-commerce is complex. The global characteristics of the Internet enable Cross-border E-commerce to meet the needs of consumers in different countries in a very direct way, with broad overseas markets and business opportunities. At the same time, goods need to be carried out across borders, even across multiple countries, in the form of flowing from the seller to the buyer. Therefore, Cross-border transactions often involve customs clearance and commodity inspection in multiple countries. It involves legal, tax, environmental protection and other requirements in local trade, relating to the selection and combination of multiple modes of transportation, thus increasing the complexity of the internal and external settings of the Cross-border E-commerce logistics industry chain.

The internal and external settings of Cross-border E-commerce influence mutually, and the elements of each species are interdependent. In Cross-border E-commerce activities, Cross-border E-commerce, Cross-border logistics, Cross-border payment and other activities cannot function independently. There are continuous exchange and interaction of goods, information or energy between each species of the ecosystem and other elements. Each element of the Cross-border ecosystem will be affected by many other elements, forming a subsystem. In this system, with a large number of subsystems cooperating with each other, it is necessary to avoid mutual consumption among subsystems and maintain the coordinated operation of all subsystems to achieve the overall value-added effect. In practice, various subsystems often fail to achieve the best cooperation. For example, Cross-border E-commerce logistics is vulnerable to the interference of trust mechanism, information transmission, transaction costs and other factors, resulting in the failure to maximize the realization of the value chain and causing an internal loss in the system. The Cross-border logistics and supply chain is the key species in the development of Cross-border E-commerce, thus forming its own ecosystem. Let's start with the participants in the logistics and supply chain section.

1.3 Participants of Cross-border E-commerce Logistics and Supply Chain

The Cross-border E-commerce logistics and supply chain is a chain-like operation series, covering procurement, warehousing and transportation, etc. As an important fulcrum in the Cross-border E-commerce industry chain, with the gradual development of the Cross-border E-commerce industry, the Cross-border

E-commerce logistics and supply chain industry has ushered in new opportunities for rapid growth.

From the perspective of physical space, the Cross-border E-commerce logistics and supply chain process is divided into exporting country logistics, international logistics and importing country logistics, which make up a supply chain, as shown in Figure 1 – 5. The transportation process of goods from the seller to the buyer is also the process of cooperation between the logistics of the exporting country (exporters) + international logistics + the logistics of the importing country (importers) , and finally completes the service for consumers. The ultimate goal of Cross-border logistics and supply chain focuses on " reducing costs, increasing efficiency, improving consumer experience " , which is a continuous and endless process. A better international logistics and supply chain means to complete a good shopping experience of consumers with lower cost, higher efficiency and better service.

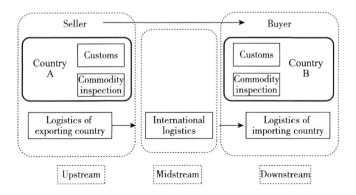

Figure 1 – 5   Cross-border E-commerce Logistics Diagram

According to Figure 1 – 5, the Cross-border E-commerce logistics and supply chain can be divided into three parts: upstream, midstream and downstream. " Upstream" refers to as " seller" , which can be suppliers and middlemen, retailers and brands. They are distributed on comprehensive Cross-border E-commerce platforms, DTC platforms, and third-party sellers on other platforms (such as social platforms, short video platforms). The mainstream Cross-border E-commerce platforms include global e-retailers such as Amazon, AliExpress, Shopify, eBay, Wish, SheIn, and regional platforms, such as Lazada, Shopee, and many local platforms in various countries. There are numerous third-party sellers who open stores on Cross-border E-commerce platforms, forming a huge group of sellers.

"Midstream" refers to Cross-border logistics and supply chain enterprise, whose operation modes are mainly classified into international commercial express, postal airmail and air parcel, Cross-border special lines and overseas warehouses, frontier warehouses, and bonded logistics in bonded areas and free trade zones, etc. It includes third-party logistics companies, as well as logistics integrators integrating third-party logistics, fourth-party logistics companies and Cross-border logistics alliances. International commercial expresses are mainly the United Parcel Service (UPS), Deutsche Post (DHL), TNT and FedEx. The postal system is extensive, and the price is preferential. The postal airmail is the main channel of international B2C fulfillment business.

"Downstream" is called "buyer", including commercial buyer (B2B) and individual buyer (B2C, C2C). It is the end user of the whole transnational logistics process, and it also tests and evaluates the effect of the whole logistics process. The quality of logistics services focuses on consumer experience, and is also the ultimate goal of the continuous development of Cross-border E-commerce logistics and supply chain. The relationship between the three is shown in Figure 1 – 6. The core logistics and supply chain connects consumers home and abroad. For example, for export Cross-border logistics, the sellers on Cross-border E-commerce platforms are consumers of logistics, and the foreign buyers on the other end are also consumers of Cross-border logistics. It is Cross-border logistics that closely links the two to achieve the best service for both parties, providing the best service at the lowest cost with the greatest efficiency.

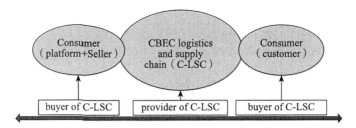

Figure 1 – 6   Cross-border E-commerce Logistics and Supply Chain Diagram

1.4   Cross-border E-commerce Logistics and Supply Chain Ecosystem

Logistics has always been the "pain point" of Cross-border E-commerce, which restricts the smooth development of Cross-border E-commerce. Cross-border logistics and supply chain involves not only domestic and foreign customs and commodity inspection, but also international logistics and transportation, with various factors of micro-level and macro-level setting. With the Cross-border E-commerce ecosystem as the background, the Cross-border E-commerce logistics and supply chain also forms its own ecosystem, and the factors that affect Cross-border E-commerce also jointly affect the Cross-border logistics and supply chain ecosystem.

Due to many influencing factors within the ecosystem and the difficulty of its improvement, many scholars have carried out theoretical and practical research on this issue and proposed their own models to try to improve the coordinative operation of the Cross-border logistics and supply chain ecosystem. Therefore, Cross-border logistics has become the mainstream research focus in Cross-border E-commerce, with the goal of "reducing costs and increasing efficiency", "offering better services and thus improving consumer experience".

1. 4. 1　Literature Review

Cao Wujun *et al.* (2019) proposed a Cross-border E-commerce ecosystem (See Figure 1 – 7) dominated by logistics enterprises on the basis of Figure 1 – 3. The logistics-oriented Cross-border E-commerce ecosystem was unity with logistics enterprises and Cross-border E-commerce platforms as the core species, combining supportive species, critical species, parasitic species and internal and external environment. Logistics enterprises and Cross-border E-commerce were closely combined to form the core and maintain the operation of Cross-border E-commerce ecosystem. It emphasized the importance of logistics enterprises and classified them as a core species.

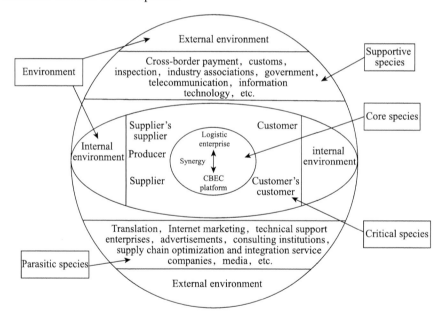

Figure 1 – 7　Integrated Cross-border E-commerce Ecosystem

Led by Logistics Enterprise

The logistics-oriented ecosystem may also be differently constructed from different perspectives. Xie Sixing and Yin Bingjie (2019) put the construction of

Cross-border logistics ecosystem in the context of Sino-US trade frictions, and proposed that Cross-border E-commerce was a comprehensive fluid system involving the participation of government, finance, commerce, communications and other parties. In order to solve the problems of logistics and supply chain, it was necessary to build creatively a smart logistics ecosystem based on the convergence of basic operations, information platforms, industrial alliance, etc.

Based on the symbiosis of technology and Cross-border E-commerce logistics and supply chain, Zhu Geng *et al.* (2018) combined Cross-border E-commerce and Cross-border logistics ecosystem, and used AI technology to interpret Cross-border logistics and supply chain. With Cross-border E-commerce logistics as the core and artificial intelligence as the support, a Cross-border E-commerce logistics and supply chain ecosystem is built. The development of AI is subjected to five elements: digital economy, platform economy, logistics economy, trade economy, and financial economy. They worked coordinately as pillars for the development of AI. The author suggested developing the segmentation function of the five pillars in high quality, and trying to form gradually a quality, efficient and deeply integrated value chain, supply chain and ecological chain. The whole process reflected a chain thinking pattern and integration thinking model.

In a word, the logistics ecosystem is a complex network system composed of logistics enterprises' living organisms and related living environments such as information technology and Internet technology (Xue Xiaofang and Li Xue, 2017). It integrates information flow with goods flow, logistics flow and capital flow to form a closed loop system of sustainable collaborative circulation, and focuses more on the general development of the entire chain (Zhang Yingchuan, 2015).

1.4.2   Reconstruction of Cross-border Logistics and Supply Chain Ecosystem

On the basis of previous studies, this chapter reconstructs the Cross-border E-commerce logistics and supply chain ecosystem, as shown in Figure 1 – 8.

Similarly, it is also composed of supportive species, core species, key species, peripheral species and Macro-setting. Let's take export as an example. Its core species is Cross-border E-commerce logistics and supply chain, which relies on the logistics and supply chain platform to connect consumers at both ends: Cross-border E-commerce platforms (including sellers on the platform, producers and suppliers for the sellers, etc.) and overseas consumers. Cross-border payment enterprises are supportive species. Cross-border marketing, technical support, advertising and consulting are peripheral species. They make up a micro-level internal setting of Cross-border logistics and supply chain. Cross-border E-commerce logistics and supply chain is subject to the same macro-level external setting as Cross-border E-commerce, that is, PESTEL factors. This is also the framework of this book. On this basis, we will discuss the challenges, risks, management and optimization of logistics and supply chain in Cross-border E-commerce.

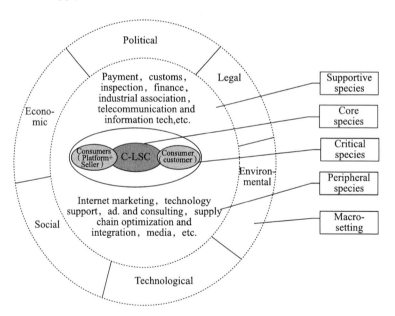

Figure 1 – 8　Cross-border Logistics and Supply Chain Ecosystem

1. 5   Collaboration Between Cross-border E-commerce and Logistics and Supply Chain

Cross-border E-commerce and Cross-border logistics and supply chain are highly related, and they are interdependently, complementarily and coordinatively working together. Cross-border E-commerce and Cross-border logistics and supply chain, as the two main bodies connecting the production and consumption in the Cross-border E-commerce industry chain, are consistent in customer demand orientation. All segments of the logistics and supply chain are serving Cross-border E-commerce, and the market expansion of Cross-border E-commerce will also influence the operation of the logistics and supply chain.

1. 5. 1   Cross-border E-commerce is Catalytic to Logistics and Supply Chain

With the rise of E-commerce, the logistics and supply chain has taken on a more demanding task. Cross-border E-commerce companies are high-tech business, and they are closely integrated with logistics and supply chain activities. That is to say, logistics and supply chain will naturally be high-tech business, too. The strong demand on logistics and supply chain generated by Cross-border E-commerce has led to a significant increase in logistics activities. In addition, the continuous development of Cross-border E-commerce boosts the logistics and supply chain to develop towards a model of networking, intelligence and integration. Logistics enterprises are forced to reduce costs, improve logistics efficiency and enhance consumer experience in the process of logistics transportation.

The joint development of E-commerce enterprises and logistics enterprises is of great significance to the optimization and development of E-commerce logistics and supply chain (Placzek,2010). This joint development is reflected in that the development of Cross-border E-commerce has also enabled international logistics-related companies to expand the source and number of customers. Logistics activities also promote the resource integration of commodity flows generated by Cross-border E-commerce. Operators and overseas consumer groups scattered across the country form a trade network through the links of the logistics system.

China's Cross-border E-commerce has a strong momentum of development. From January to July 2022, the total import and export volume reached 23.6 trillion *yuan*, up 10.4% year on year. Accordingly, the import and export volume of China's Cross-border E-commerce in 2022 was 2.11 trillion *yuan*, up 9.8%. The Cross-border E-commerce has an obvious positive effect on the Cross-border logistics industry, and the two basically maintain synchronous growth, as shown in Figure 1 – 9. The development of Cross-border E-commerce provides better market opportunities for logistics and supply chain, and its level of development has also become a key factor in the integration of logistics chain (Xiang Jixiu,2021). The logistics industry needs to optimize and upgrade its industrial structure to meet the requirements of Cross-border E-commerce, and actively seek improvement in the

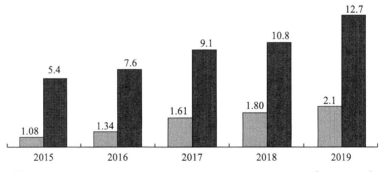

■ Market size of China's Cross-border E-commerce logistics industry (unit:trillion)
■ Scale of Cross-border E-commerce transactions in China (unit:trillion)

Figure 1 –9　The Pulling Effect of Cross-border E-commerce

on Cross-border Logistics

aspects of clustering, informatization and digitalization to achieve the overall improvement of Cross-border logistics and supply chain.

1.5.2　Cross-border Logistics and Supply Chain Supports Cross-border E-commerce

At the beginning of 2023, the pandemic had been brought under control. Under the background of global economic recession, consumer demand goes into the weak side which brings certain challenges to China's Cross-border E-commerce. Under the influence of these factors, Cross-border E-commerce needs a more complete and integrative logistics and supply chain to improve consumer experience in order to go through the hard economic cycle and achieve a long-term, healthy and sustainable development. With the continuous growth of China's Cross-border E-commerce sales volume, the importance of Cross-border logistics and supply chain is increasing. Demands for the correlation and coordination between the two are going to be higher, especially on the development scale and efficiency of Cross-border logistics and supply chain. As for the supporting role of Cross-border logistics for Cross-border E-commerce, domestic scholars have roughly achieved a consensus, as a large number of Cross-border E-commerce transactions need to be realized ultimately through logistics activities(Su Hang,2017). An integrative and digitalized application of international logistics mode can effectively support the development of Cross-border E-commerce industry.

At present, Cross-border logistics and supply chain has become the core competitiveness for Cross-border E-commerce. From the perspective of logistics itself, logistics quality is an important indicator of the quality of Cross-border E-commerce development. The timeliness and guaranteed quality of logistics are important indicators that affect overseas customer satisfaction with Cross-border E-commerce transactions (Wang Yunan,2022).

From the perspective of user experience, in the past two decades, the Cross-border E-commerce platform has been continuously optimized, the transaction volume has gradually increased, and the categories have expanded continuously. For consumers, the front-end platform is beautifully and conveniently designed and presented, the product quality is relatively high, and process of transaction is convenient and speedy, which meet most of their consumption needs. With the development of E-commerce, online consumers are more concerned about the timeliness of logistics (the time span from goods ordering to receiving). The efficiency and service quality of Cross-border logistics have become main factors affecting the sales of Cross-border E-commerce enterprises (Li Hang and Huang Xinyi, 2021).

If the development of core competitiveness is insufficient to promote the development of Cross-border E-commerce, it will become the "pain point" of Cross-border E-commerce development. However, the cost reduction and efficiency boost of Cross-border logistics are closely related to its own complexity, which is a long-term and arduous task.

1.6　Characteristics of Cross-border E-commerce Logistics and Supply Chain

Unlike the domestic logistics and supply chain network, the Cross-border E-commerce logistics and supply chain is more complex, which involves many knots and chains. There are more risks in every segment and thus it is riskier. So, the coordination of various stages is more challenging.

1.6.1　Long and Complex Industrial Chain

The long distance, time length, high cost, complex process and poor controllability of Cross-border E-commerce logistics are the substantial disparities between Cross-border logistics and domestic logistics. In Cross-border logistics, the first-leg transportation can be composed of sea transport, land transport, air transport, and special line, etc. Xue Lei *et al.* (2022) divided the whole structure of the Cross-border logistics and supply chain into seven sections, namely front-end collection, warehousing and sorting, customs declaration, nation-to-nation trunk transportation, customs clearance, overseas warehousing, and last mile fulfillment. The seven parts can also be divided into two major modules, namely, domestic transportation and overseas transportation. From parcel collection to customs declaration, they can be generally referred to as the domestic section; and from customs clearance to final delivery, they can be roughly referred to as the overseas section. Comparing with the logistics sections of traditional international trade, Cross-border E-commerce logistics includes domestic commodity collection and sorting at the domestic end, and final fulfillment to customers at the overseas end. It needs to coordinate the "first mile" parcel collection part and the "last mile" distribution part into a whole procedure. Therefore, the Cross-border logistics and supply chain needs to coordinate more segments, and the whole chain is more complex. Unlike traditional international trade, Cross-border E-commerce requires high logistics timeliness, which is not only the timeliness of goods distribution, but also the timeliness of goods return and exchange. From this point of view, Cross-border logistics has a great demand for air transport mode, but the price is generally high, which is contrary to the characteristics of large quantity of Cross-border E-commerce products and low unit price per customer. Such contradictions restrict the efficiency improvement of Cross-border E-commerce logistics. What is more, these contradictions are mainly reflected in Cross-border logistics: First, the efficiency of the last mile delivery is low. There are few logistics enterprises that have built their own "last mile" overseas fulfillment center. It is necessary for Cross-border logistics enterprises to actively integrate and cooperate with overseas delivery resources to localize the final delivery services. In this way, they can improve consumer experience and provide better services. Second, the return and exchange of goods are not timely. From the perspective of customer, a large proportion of logistics needs are individual customers. These needs are end-to-end, of small-batch, of multi-batch, and of high-frequency for goods return and exchange. Customers usually expect the return and exchange process for Cross-border E-commerce to match the efficiency of domestic E-commerce, which is difficult to achieve given the lengthy and complex nature of Cross-border supply chain.

1.6.2 Difficulty in Integrating the Resources of the Whole Chain

At present, there are only a few Cross-border logistics enterprises that can effectively penetrate into both upstream and downstream business and provide end-to-end services as fourth-party logistics, logistics integrators or logistics alliances. The differences in political and economic systems among countries, consumer culture and consumption habits, the influence of geopolitics, the consumer psychology in the post-pandemic era, the establishment of regional economies and other factors (that are not conducive to global economic integration) come one after another, deeply affecting the establishment, maintenance and consolidation of Cross-border E-commerce logistics and supply chain. At present, China's Cross-border E-commerce logistics and supply chain is still characterized by its fragmentation. The servicing area is relatively scattered, the degree of resource sharing is low, the development is uneven, and the degree of resource integration is low, resulting in high logistics costs. The logistics environment, customs, economic development level and national culture are very different around the world. The difficulty coefficient of Cross-border logistics is doubled compared with that of domestic logistics (Mu Yanping, 2015).

1. 6. 3   Unbalanced Regional Development

China's Cross-border logistics and supply chain is mainly located in the southeast coastal areas, with less competition coming from the central and western regions. Most logistics companies are operating on a small scale. Logistics industry is highly dispersed. Due to the strong economy in the Pearl River Delta, the Yangtze River Delta and the Bohai Rim, the demand for Cross-border logistics transportation is strong, and the infrastructure of shipping, railway, road and air transportation in these regions is relatively complete. Therefore, the supply and competition of transportation resources is intense. While in the central and western regions, due to a relatively inactive economy, low demand for Cross-border transport, high transport costs and less investment in international freight service resources, logistics is less developed. Among them, the competition is characterized by regionalism and industry separation. The degree of competition is limited by its own financial strength, management and technical capabilities, as well as the separation of China's logistics market and other factors. Competition exists within regions, industries or enterprises. For example, competition exists among Cross-border logistics companies in the Yangtze River Delta; Or the competition of resources exists between a certain industry, such as 3C industry, electronic product manufacturing industry, etc. On the contrary, there is less competition across regions and industries. With the increasing demand for Cross-border E-commerce, most Cross-border logistics companies have shifted from providing single transportation service to diversified services, such as cooperation with overseas warehousing companies, to provide first-leg customs clearance, warehousing, distribution, as well as many derivative and alternative services related to FBA in the chain of Cross-border logistics, such as label making and replacing, one parcel delivery service, etc.

Chapter 2   Cross-border Logistics and Supply Chain Mode and Enhancement Philosophy

This chapter focuses on logistics and supply chain modes in Cross-border logistics and supply chain practice, as well as the risks and problems, concept, strategy, business operation and final goal in the process of optimization.

International logistics mode in Cross-border E-commerce refers to what channels are used to complete the distribution of Cross-border goods. Cross-border E-commerce international logistics and supply chain is generally completed with the help of third-party logistics. Some Cross-border E-commerce platforms are aware of the importance of logistics and supply chain and begin to build their own logistics and supply chain system. For instance, the domestic section of AliExpress logistics is established on the basis of Cainiao network and its global distribution is conducted by combining China Post international express and postal system of other countries around the world. Cainiao also established its special line. The "5-day delivery" international express program was initiated jointly by Cainiao and AliExpress in 2023, targeting the markets of Britain, the Netherlands, Spainish, Belgium and the Republic of Korea. DTC platform SheIn, in order to meet its fast fashion features, has established its own logistics and supply chain system. Amazon has established its own mature FBA logistics and distribution system to achieve efficient logistics and supply chain management with overseas warehouses. However, a commonly-observed rule is that the cost of construction and maintenance for logistics and supply chain is very high, and the cycle of getting revenue from its venture capital's initial investment is long. Though Amazon has established its own mature FBA fulfillment system, the high cost of running the system, the need to invest a lot of money at the start-up stage, long profit cycle are drawbacks of logistics operation, which result in the cost rise of FBA logistics and warehousing[1], and bring a lot of pressure on sellers. In general, China's Cross-border logistics is dominated by China Post + third-party logistics. The continuous emergence of fourth-party logistics, as well as logistics integrators and Cross-border logistics alliances, is being conceived, representing the future direction of Cross-border logistics and supply chain.

2. 1   Cross-border E-commerce International Logistics and Supply Chain Mode

At present, the main modes of Cross-border logistics include China Post air mail and air parcel, international commercial express, overseas warehouse, international logistics special line, frontier warehouse, bonded area and free trade zone logistics, etc. These modes cooperate with each other to fulfill the function of logistics and supply chain.

2. 1. 1   China Post Air Mail and Air Parcel

China Post Air Mail and Air Parcel works as the main Channel for China's Cross-border logistics, which fulfills the import and export of E-commerce goods

---

[1]   https://www. sohu. com/a/542139104_115514, 20 - 2 - 2023.

with the help of Universal Postal Union. According to statistics, more than 70% of China's current Cross-border E-commerce goods are transported through postal system, of which China Post occupies about 50% share[1]. In the international postal parcel service, China Post, Hong Kong Post, Belgium Post, Russia Post and Germany Post are the popular options. The postal network has a wide coverage, low price and convenient customs clearance. However, long duration of transportation, sometimes a high rate of loss for regular parcels, and the problem of no tracking for non-registered pieces are obvious. There are limitations in measurement, weight and shape of goods. In practice, the logistics channel of China Post is more suitable for B2C retail goods of low value and parcels of small size.

2. 1. 2　International Commercial Express

International Commercial express mainly refers to UPS, FedEx, DHL, TNT which are also called the big four commercial courier giants. International express has prominent advantages like large transportation and strong distribution capacity, fast speed, good customer experience, and on the other hand, a high price (Cao Wujun *et al*. , 2019). For example, if a parcel is sent from China to the United States by using UPS, it can arrive within 48 hours at the earliest. In addition, China's local express companies are also gradually involved in Cross-border logistics and supply chain business, such as SF Express, [2]STO Express (or ShenTong Express) and so on. Different International expresses can be selected for different customer groups considering various factors: such as location of a country, commodity type, volume size, commodity weight, etc. to achieve the fast delivery of goods through different channels. In short, international express delivery has the advantages of high timeliness and low loss rate, but the price is relatively high, especially

---

① https://www. cifnews. com/article/85581? ivk_sa = 1024320u,20 – 1 – 2023.

② https://baijiahao. baidu. com/s? id = 1704786789979882738&wfr = spider&for = pc, 20 – 1 – 2023.

in remote areas, and the surcharge is even higher. Another disadvantage is that sometimes high-voltage electronic products and goods of irregular shapes are not accepted for delivery.

2. 1. 3　Overseas Warehouse

Overseas warehouse is a hot cake in Cross-border logistics and supply chain and it enjoys policy support at present in China. Firstly, overseas warehouses is leased or built in the consumer countries. The procedure goes like this: the seller firstly sends goods to overseas warehouses for stocking through first-leg transportation, then sells goods through Cross-border E-commerce platforms, and then delivers them directly from overseas warehouses after receiving customer orders. Overseas warehouses could be built or leased by Cross-border E-commerce platforms. And in practice, they are often built or leased by third-party logistics enterprises, and platforms work with enterprises by the way of cooperation. For instance, Amazon, eBay and other Cross-border E-commerce platforms have officially launched their overseas warehouses in the way of cooperation with local enterprises. Chinese third-party logistics enterprises such as SF Express and other logistics companies are also gradually involved in the overseas warehouse business in some mature markets.

Overseas warehouse is considered as the innovation and breakthrough of Cross-border logistics and supply chain, which is expected to make up for the shortcomings of international postal services and international commercial express in the following aspects, such as logistics efficiency, logistics cost, customs and commodity inspection, localization, goods return and exchange, etc. However, the leasing, construction and operation of overseas warehouses require a huge investment in the early stage, and the profit cycle is as long as 10 years (For example, Amazon's profit cycle may be in 10 years, which is a challenge for venture capital investment①). Besides, the location and size of overseas warehouses are also big issues to be considered, which require separate legal entities to operate and professional personnel and capital. In the operation of overseas warehouse, an accurate sales expectation before the pre-shipment of goods will be as important. Otherwise, there would generate a lot of sales problems. After the first-leg transportation, it would lead to an increased storage costs and thus squeeze profits due to stagnant sales and inventory or even backlog.

2. 1. 4 International Logistics Special Line

When the volume of goods reaches a certain stable scale, international logistics special line is a good choice. International logistics special line is a Cross-border special delivery method for a specific country or region. The starting point, destination, transportation means, transportation route and time schedule are basically fixed. Transportation time is shorter than international postal parcel, logistics cost is lower than international express, and customs clearance is guaranteed due to special arrangement. For Cross-border E-commerce of fixed routes, it is a better logistics solution. However, international logistics special line is limited to certain regions and quantities, which are the drawbacks of this mode. The special line mainly includes air line, marine line, railroad line, continental bridge line and fixed multimodal line. The most famous railroad line is China Railway Express running from China to Europe, YanWen logistics operates its line to Russia and the same goes to SF Shenzhen – Taipei all-cargo routes②.

---

① Amazon Empire: The Rise and Reign of Jeff Bezos [EB/OL]. [2023 – 01 – 20]. https://www. bilibili. com/video/av93595636/.

② http://www. taihainet. com/news/twnews/bilateral/2015 – 03 – 23/1383416. html, 20 – 1 – 2023.

2. 1. 5   Frontier Warehouse

Frontier warehouse refers to leasing or building warehouses within the borders of neighboring countries of Cross-border E-commerce destination countries. The seller would deliver goods to the warehouses in advance, and then ship from the frontier warehouse after getting customer orders on platforms. According to different geographical locations, the frontier warehouse can be absolute frontier warehouse and relative frontier warehouse. Absolute frontier warehouse is usually built around the seller's city and is adjacent to the buyer's country, such as the case of China and Russia. The warehouse is set up in Harbin or a Chinese city along the border. Relative frontier warehouse means that when the two parties of transactions are not adjacent to each other, the warehouse will be located in the border city of the buyer's adjacent country. For example, China's Cross-border E-commerce transactions to Brazil. Warehouses are set up in adjacent border cities of Argentina, Paraguay, Peru and other bordering countries. For the buyer, it is relative frontier warehouse, and for the seller, it is overseas warehouse. The operation of overseas warehouses requires high costs. There is a risk of goods backlog, and it is difficult to return the goods to the home country once delivered. All these factors promote the development of absolute frontier warehouses, such as the frontier warehouse set up in Harbin conducting parcels mainly to Russia. On the other hand, because of the instability in tax policies and political situation, currency devaluation and serious inflation in some countries, these factors stimulate the emergence of frontier warehouses. For example, Brazil's tax policies are very strict, and the cost of overseas warehouses is very high. Setting up frontier warehouses at its bordering countries and then making use of South American's Mercosur (a free trade agreement) to promote Cross-border E-commerce to Brazil is a way to reduce costs and improve efficiency.

2. 1. 6　Bonded Area and Free Trade Zone Logistics

Due to China's unique industrial advantages, trade environment and promotion policies, China's foreign trade business especially importing business uses bonded area or Free Trade Zone (FTZ) logistics. It means that the would-be imported goods is firstly delivered to the bonded area or FTZ warehouses, and after obtaining customer orders through the Cross-border E-commerce platform, goods would be sorted and packed in the bonded area or free trade zone warehouses, and then they would go through transportation, distribution, delivery and final fulfillment. This mode could make use of the benefits of consolidation logistics and scale economics, which is conducive to shortening logistics time and reducing logistics costs. For example, Amazon takes China (Shanghai) Pilot Free Trade Zone as the entrance and introduces global commodity lines. Usually, Cross-border E-commerce enterprises can first put the goods in the FTZ. After customers place orders, the platform would send the goods out from FTZ, and thus effectively shorten the delivery time. Through the storage in bonded area or FTZ, its comprehensive advantages and preferential measures can be effectively utilized, especially the convenience in logistics, customs clearance, commodity inspection, collection and payment of foreign exchange and tax refund. It would simplify the operation of Cross-border E-commerce and realize the purpose of promoting Cross-border E-commerce transactions.

2. 2　Participants of Cross-border Logistics and Supply Chain

At present, the Cross-border E-commerce logistics and supply chain is generally undertaken by third-party logistics companies or fourth-party companies as the main organizers to complete the circulation of goods. Specifically, the actual operation of the Cross-border logistics and supply chain is mainly completed by third-party logistics companies. It is the professional third-party logistics enterprises other than buyers and sellers who are undertaking logistics services in the form of service outsourcing and contract commissioning. Though it is relatively easy for domestic E-merchants to build their own logistics, the Cross-border E-commerce logistics and supply chain is much more complex and requires high logistics investment. Although big Cross-border E-commerce platforms try to build their own logistics systems, most Cross-border platforms and sellers choose third-party logistics model considering factors of capital, the complexity of Cross-border logistics and various macro-setting factors. They often have a cooperation with postal and international courier companies. Sometimes, postal service or international commercial express companies prefer to cooperate with local third-party logistics companies for last mile delivery in some countries and regions. Cross-border logistics connect in a variety of modes to fulfill logistics services. Or, the fourth-party logistics companies take the initiative to build a platform, and the third-party logistics companies work as functional service providers to complete the distribution of goods. A large number of domestic and international marine transportation and international freight forwarding enterprises have rich experience in import and export, overseas business operation, overseas business network layout and international operation ability. They are the partners for Cross-border E-commerce and Cross-border logistics and supply chain.

Fourth-party logistics companies are organizations that provide logistics planning, consulting, logistics information systems, supply chain management and other activities for both sides of the transaction and third-party logistics. They provide integrated and comprehensive supply chain solutions by deploying and managing the resources, capabilities and technologies of themselves and other service providers with complementary capabilities (Zhao Guanghua, 2014). The advantage of the fourth-party logistics lies in its resource integration capability. Through the influence of the entire supply chain, it integrates all kinds of social resources on the basis of enterprise logistics solution, and realizes logistics information sharing and full utilization of social logistics resources. Excellent fourth-party logistics can integrate logistics and distribution service resources around the world and provide services such as open price comparison bidding, global intelligent path optimization, multi-logistics providers collaborative distribution, automatic order following, and big data intelligent analysis. Though there is great complexity in Cross-border E-commerce and Cross-border logistics, China's fourth-party logistics companies emerge, injecting fresh forces into Cross-border logistics.

No matter they are the third-party logistics companies or the fourth-party logistics companies, when importing, they can use direct mail, duty – paid import and other methods. When exporting, for the purpose of cost saving, they use consolidation logistics, that is, logistics companies would collect all goods to native or local storage centers first. After reaching a certain quantity, they transport goods to overseas buyers through international logistics companies. Or, logistics companies gather goods from China first, and then distribute these goods in bulk to the world. Additionally, some Cross-border E-commerce enterprises with similar product categories would establish a strategic alliance and set up a common Cross-border logistics operation center, using the concept of scale economy or complementary economy to achieve the purpose of reducing costs. For example, Milanoo. com (a Chengdu-based Cross-border E-commerce company built in 2008) has built its own warehousing centers in Guangzhou and Chengdu, and after the goods are gathered in the warehousing centers, they are sent to foreign buyers through international express.

2. 3   Problems of Cross-border Logistics and Supply Chain Mode

2. 3. 1   Small Scale and Huge Regional Differences

At present, most of the functional logistics companies in each logistics mode are small in scale, with small-and medium-sized logistics and supply chain companies in the majority. Their business scope is generally narrow. The development of domestic logistics regions is unbalanced, and the regional differences in foreign logistics are huge. With the development of international trade and Cross-border E-commerce, the number of China's logistics companies is gradually increasing, and they are mainly located in Yangtze River Delta, Pearl River Delta, Bohai Rim Economic Zone and other economically developed areas. As a matter of fact, there is a large gap between the number of Cross-border logistics companies in the inland western regions and that of coastal areas. As to the business scope and capacity of Chinese logistics, compared with international commercial express, there is a huge gap. Even the total business volume of China's top ten international logistics companies is still in its infancy stage compared to the top four international express companies. China Ocean Shipping Logistics, China Railway Express, China Post Logistics, Deppon Logistics, China Storage and Development Co. , Ltd. and Southern Logistics Group, with a state-owned background, have a large gap with foreign commercial expresses in terms of operation methods and efficiency. There is a great potential in developing information system and value concept of logistics. In both import and export logistics, each platform has different logistics service companies with different transportation and distribution efficiency. In addition to that, the stability, flexibility and quick response capability of logistics and supply chain are greatly affected by political environment, economic environment, transportation routes, social events (such as strikes and conflicts), etc. Besides, the after-sales service is slow, and shopping experience still has more room for development. In regions with high business volume such as Europe and America, logistics transportation and distribution are much more efficient. While in places of low business volume and less economically developed regions, logistics service is poor. The gap between the two is large. In brief, the main bottleneck of logistics is still high cost and low efficiency. Shopping service and experience are to be improved.

2. 3. 2　Scattered Logistics Modes and Poor Network

The various international logistics modes mentioned above perform the function of transportation and distribution in their respective areas, and the business volume is small compared with the foreign logistics business volume (such as the number of delivered parcels), the capacity level is limited, and the automation level of transportation and sorting is low and scattered. If each logistics company designs its own logistics and supply chain system to cover as many regions and countries as possible, the capital and resources are thinly divided and scattered, resulting in a waste of resources and a low overall level of network systems and a serious overlap in development. The information flow in logistics companies and in logistics modes cannot be shared, which is costly and inefficient.

The current logistics mode is mixed and overlapped in business and resources. On the one hand, it has so many sections to integrate, and processes are complex. on the other hand, the development level of logistics varies. It is difficult to use one single logistics mode throughout the whole process, and the efficiency of a combined mode is low. The integration ability still needs to be enhanced. The future logistics and supply chain should strengthen its integration ability and develop differentiated services, rather than the coexistence of multiple modes, which is not conducive to efficiency improvement. In addition, in the contact process with local companies, there are problems like rising costs caused by poor network chain, information system that could not be shared and interest conflicts of each party that could not be balanced.

2. 3. 3   Low-Level Thinking Mode and Value Chain Concept

Integrating logistics and supply chain with value chain concept is a long-term development goal. For example, in the logistics outsourcing mode, with the help of third-party local logistics to start the "last mile" distribution, the quality of service varies widely. Fourth-party logistics companies need to integrate logistics resources locally, improve service level, unify service quality, promote the development of E-commerce economy and logistics industry, integrate data and basic platforms, provide differentiated and intensive supply chain solutions. In this way, the flows of logistics, commodity, capital, information will work with commodity inspection and customs clearance, thus enhancing value-adding capacity of the whole supply chain.

2. 4   Enhancement of Cross-border Logistics and Supply Chain Mode

Since Cross-border logistics has become a constraint factor affecting the future development of Cross-border E-commerce, the improvement of logistics and supply chain mode will be beneficial to the development of Cross-border E-commerce. The optimization of international logistics and supply chain is especially important to build the core competitiveness of Cross-border E-commerce. Based on the perspective of ecosystem and the actual environment of current Cross-border E-commerce development, this section will discuss the enhancement from perspectives of concept, strategy, business practice, and ultimate goal.

2. 4. 1　Enhancement Concept: Integrative Thinking

China's Cross-border E-commerce logistics has a short history of about 20 years and is still in the early stage. With the concept of integrative thinking, it needs continuous optimization and integration to achieve better development.

2. 4. 1. 1　Factual and Theoretical Basis

Compared with Cross-border E-commerce, domestic E-commerce has a mature development and ecosystem: smooth capital, logistics, information and goods flows, and thus presenting the world's largest domestic E-commerce market. Compared with domestic E-commerce, the overall development of Cross-border E-commerce in China is dispersive and relatively weak. Although the number of business entities reaches 705,000 and there are 3,014,000 employees, the proportion of enterprises with operation volume over 10 million *yuan* is less than 10%, which is still in the early stage of development in general (Qi Fei, 2020). Western Cross-border E-commerce started earlier with a broader horizon and has developed for a longer time. They made better use of the dividend period of E-commerce, and accumulated more experience and took more pioneering opportunities. With more convenient international means of payment, such as PayPal which has a strong Cross-border payment capability worldwide, platforms such as eBay and Amazon, after more than 2 decades of trial-and-error and continuous investment, have occupied a more favorable position. The world's large E-commerce markets, such as the United States and European countries, are close in terms of institutional distance, cultural distance, consumption habits, economic development levels, etc. They have the priority of exploring each other's market and enjoy the first mover advantage.

Western E-commerce companies such as Amazon have better logistics and distribution capabilities. In addition, the four major commercial expresses started early, with more capital investment and advanced concepts. They have a great development by occupying the main market of international commercial logistics. In contrast, China's Cross-border E-commerce logistics service resources are scattered, and the market concentration rate is relatively low. Postal air mail is currently the mainstream international logistics distribution mode, which indicates that we don't have strong influence in international logistics market. In order to improve the international logistics distribution capacity, we have to use the four major international commercial expresses and other logistics channels to complete the operation of the supply chain and efficient distribution. However, the high cost of international commercial express and the low value of Chinese goods are not always balanced. Commercial express is more suitable for high-end items with high value and small size, which imposes a greater pressure on the retail goods with low average order value and is not conducive to cost reducing. Despite the prevalence of the two mainstream logistics modes—post service and commercial express— these two modes are limited in either slow speed, small transportation volume or high cost, which are not conducive to enhancing the competitiveness of China's international logistics and the development of logistics and supply chain. At present, the development of third-party domestic logistics and supply chain is mainly driven by multinational companies and concentrates in certain industries such as railroad, grain, home appliances, electronics and automobile industry chain (Du Zhiping, 2020). In a word, the development of China's Cross-border E-commerce logistics industry chain is still in the primary stage.

According to the life cycle theory, the development stages of enterprises and industries include budding, development, growth, maturity and decline, and different stages of the life cycle match different organizational management modes and business modes. As an important support and critical part for the development of Cross-border E-commerce, Cross-border logistics and supply chain is constrained to the life cycle of Cross-border E-commerce and the life cycle of logistics and supply chain. Therefore, logistics enterprises should first know their own life cycle in order to get a better development mode of Cross-border logistics. Since 2017, China's Cross-border E-commerce Gross Merchandise Volume (GMV) has increased nearly 10 times in 5 years, and the Cross-border E-commerce industry has entered a period of rapid development. The Cross-border E-commerce logistics and supply chain industry is still in the early stage of development with scattered resources, low market concentration and low resource utilization. Statistics of the National Development and Reform Commission show that in 2021, the ratio of China's total social logistics costs to GDP was 14. 6% , with a 3. 4% reduction from 2012. Although the gap with major Western economies is narrowing, there is still a significant gap, and it is difficult to close the gap in a short time. Therefore, the *14th Five-Year Plan for the Development of Modern Logistics* is to "promote logistics quality, efficiency and cost reduction" and consider that as an important task of the 14th Five-Year Plan. It clearly puts forward the goal of logistics: by 2025, the ratio of total social logistics costs to GDP will be reduced by about 2% compared with 2020. For the better development of logistics and supply chain, it needs to rely on a good macro environment and strong integration ability. This is the challenge of the whole logistics industry, as well as the opportunity of logistics development. Cross-border logistics also faces the same challenges and opportunities.

In practice, integration is an inherent requirement for the development of enterprises and industries. Enterprises must face the changing market and customer needs. What's more, the macro environment and micro environment are in constant change. Enterprise top management must adapt to the internal and external environment to meet changes actively. Consumers prefer better consumer experience, efficient after-sales service, environmentally friendly packaging and lower prices. The company's products need to be updated constantly to meet the needs and create different demands. The integration of elements within the enterprise can release more space for cost and efficiency and provide better logistics solutions. The development of industry is limited by the external environment. Changes in the macro environment are sometimes difficult to control, such as natural disasters, worldwide pandemics, political conflicts, trade frictions, geopolitics, regional economic integration, anti-globalization waves, etc. All these bring drawbacks to the development of the industry. The ever-changing unfavorable factors force enterprises and industries to make structural adjustments and strategic adjustments, and to respond to changes in the internal and external environment with newer ideas. Therefore, it is necessary to have an integrative thinking.

2.4.1.2   Integrative Thinking

Integrative thinking, also known as integration thinking and holistic thinking pattern (Qi Fei, 2020), is net and chain thinking, synergistic thinking (Zhang Xiaheng and Guo Hailing, 2016; Zhang Xiaheng, 2018; Fu Shuaishuai *et al.*, 2021; Mi Yan, 2022), and holistic thinking (Wang Yunan, 2022) in the logistics and supply chain. The embodiment of the integration of logistics and supply chain means that it is necessary to integrate resources and logistics and supply chain mode, and integrate all resources in the Cross-border E-commerce system that are beneficial to logistics and supply chain from the perspective of coordinated development of supply chain and value chain. It integrates not only from the macroscopic point of view to create a favorable environment, but also from the microscopic point of view, includes integration of policies, integration of regions, integration among logistics enterprises, integration within logistics enterprises, etc. It is meaningful to use integration thinking to make long-term development planning from a bigger perspective, wider scene and more ambitious goal. Specifically, from the direction of logistics integration of Cross-border E-commerce international logistics and supply chain mode integration, international logistics mode optimization needs to pay more attention to compatibility of goods and logistics modes by taking supply chain management thought as the core to develop integrated logistics solutions and build core competitiveness of Cross-border E-commerce.

2. 4. 2 Enhancement Strategy: Integrated Logistics and Supply Chain Solution

For the enhancement of international logistics mode of Cross-border E-commerce, integrated logistics and supply chain solution is the best strategy. The competition of Cross-border E-commerce also means the competition of logistics and supply chain. So the integration and optimization of each section of the supply chain and the design of efficient logistics solutions can maximize the benefits and promote the development of Cross-border E-commerce. In the field of Cross-border E-commerce, the Cross-border E-commerce supply chain includes manufacturers, suppliers, international logistics companies, warehousing centers, distributors and foreign customers, and these elements constitute the whole network. The objects of management are the flows of goods, logistics, capital and information that are in the network. Logistics is the "bridge" in the Cross-border E-commerce supply chain, which in turn serves the whole Cross-border E-commerce supply chain. In this regard, logistics enterprises in the new era must go deeper into the end-to-end supply chain operation and innovate supply chain services to form a new business model, so as to play the supportive role of logistics in the whole supply chain.

The operations in international logistics include order taking, receiving, warehousing, sorting, forwarding, packaging, loading and unloading, as well as commodity inspection, international payment settlement, customs clearance, after-sales service, etc. These processes constitute the logistics subsystem of the overall supply chain, which involves different countries and different international logistics enterprises. In view of this, the awareness of synergy of each logistics nodes in the international supply chain of Cross-border E-commerce should be strengthened, and the choice of logistics mode should integrate each section of the supply chain and strengthen the correlation, synergy and support among each part.

2. 4. 3   Enhancement of Business Practice: Micro Aspect and Macro Aspect

The down-to-earth business practice and operation of Cross-border E-commerce logistics and supply chain can be carried out from two aspects: micro aspect and macro aspect.

2. 4. 3. 1   Micro Operation

Firstly, the systematization and integration of each section and the procedure of logistics. All sections including warehousing, distribution, packaging, trans-shipment, loading and unloading, after-sales service, goods return and exchange, commodity inspection, international payment settlement, customs clearance should be systematized. Some nodal issues like Cross-border transportation, customs clearance, are the problems that logistics enterprises must convincingly solve so that they can develop customized and optimal logistics solutions. For either a third-party logistics or a fourth-party logistics enterprise, it will be a long-term sustainable task to cultivate the core competitiveness in response to the market situation.

Secondly, the informationization of logistics and supply chain. An international logistics service platform needs to be informationalized. Informatization is an internal requirement of Cross-border E-commerce international logistics integration, and the construction of a unified information platform is an effective way to achieve Cross-border E-commerce logistics inter-connection. With the changes in the demand of Cross-border logistics center, the integration of order taking, receiving, warehousing, forwarding, packaging, loading and unloading, commodity inspection, international settlement and customs clearance requires the construction of a unified information platform for Cross-border E-commerce logistics to meet the information collection needs of various functional departments in logistics enterprises. The integration also includes internal inventory management, information systems and distribution systems of logistics enterprises. The information tracking of Cross-border logistics should be transparent, traceable and accurate in the whole process. All in all, the integration of information is the basis of logistics, and the information technology built on the trust mechanism should reach manufacturers and warehouses and deeply connect consumers, which is the guarantee of Cross-border logistics integration.

Thirdly, refinement on the combination and permutation of logistics modes. Refinement of logistics modes means that the characteristics of the product, timeliness, cost and other different conditions should be considered in a comprehensive and sustainable way. The selection of logistics providers not only should be based on the logistics enterprise's past experience, service and its strengths, but also should precisely match external macro factors for the purpose of offering a low cost and high efficiency international logistics model. On the other hand, differentiated and customerized services will be a more sensible choice. That is, the cost and efficiency of logistics could go through the test from the market, and providing consumers with choices of differentiated logistics services will be more in line with the current situation.

Finally, service localization and overseas warehouse. In order to provide better services, localization is the ultimate solution of Cross-border logistics development. Overseas warehouse is one of the specific performances of localization service. Therefore, Chinese government promotes vigorously the construction of overseas warehouse and encourages third-party logistics enterprises to build or lease overseas warehouse. Overseas warehouses can reduce transportation costs, accelerate delivery speed, and localize sales and distribution to improve consumer's shopping experience. Overseas warehouses will be the mainstream of international logistics mode for Cross-border E-commerce logistics (Pang Yan, 2015; Ji Fang and Zhang Xiaheng, 2015; Qi Fei, 2020). However, the construction of overseas warehouse requires a huge amount of capital investment, a great amount of orders and a good globalized economy as the background. Under the context of global economic downturn, E-commerce business declined at the end of 2022. E-commerce platforms laid off some workers and their business shrunk. Facing the fluctuations of US dollars, ever-increasing risks and cautious venture capital investment, there is a decrease of risk tolerance for overseas warehouse. Enterprises are cautious in building new ones and some are scaling down their business. Moreover, overseas warehouse is more suitable for a powerful Cross-border E-commerce industry and big third-party logistics enterprises. The small-and medium-sized Cross-border sellers are in a poor situation who could only rely on other big logistics companies to form an alliance and to achieve better integration effect. In short, the economic environment is the foundation for the development of overseas warehouses. Only when there are great signs of global economic development could the construction of overseas warehouse have a great development and thus promote the industry of Cross-border E-commerce.

2. 4. 3. 2   Macro Operation

First of all, logistics readjustments under integration thinking means that big enterprises could provide integrating solutions. That is, the enterprises are more capable of integrating the external logistics resources. In other words, it means the integrating capability of upstream, midstream and downstream supply chain resources. Specifically, it can be performed by logistics integrator, fourth-party logistics or Cross-border logistics alliance. Whether it is a logistics integrator or a logistics alliance with the fourth-party logistics as the core, it is all about the integration of resources and the efficient resource utilization of the whole supply chain, emphasizing the synergistic development of each participant (Ji Fang and Zhang Xiaheng, 2015; Mi Yan, 2022), forming a symbiosis and development of the internal ecosystem. On the one hand, the supply chain of production, logistics, sales and consumers is integrated and systematized, which means that producers, Cross-border E-commerce platform and consumers are connected. On the other hand, logistics, capital flow and information flow are unified to form a trust group.

Secondly, the supply chain management works as the core of customized integrated logistics solutions. Under the promotion of informationization and globalization, the upgrading of industrial chain promotes the transformation of supply chain further to integrated services. International logistics enterprises need to sort out systematically the changes in logistics demand at each node of the supply chain, and form a new logistics service system of supply chain integration through process re-engineering and logistics resource integration. Construction of international logistics network synergy system should be based on value chain theory. The integrated logistics solutions are to strengthen the international logistics network synergy, especially the synergy of logistics nodes, and to encourage experienced logistics companies to establish independent overseas warehouses.

Thirdly, a good international environment is in urgent need. Globalization is the perfect environment for the development of Cross-border E-commerce. Under the effects of anti-global factors, the 6 macro factors (political, economic, social, technological, environmental, legal) of Cross-border logistics and supply chain ecosystem are especially important in today's situation. If micro factors such as technology and information systems are the "water" needed for Cross-border E-commerce development, the macro environment is the "air" for Cross-border E-commerce development. The GMV of Cross-border E-commerce at the end of 2022 once again showed the huge impact of changes in macro factors on the development of Cross-border E-commerce. For example, the protection of Intellectual Property Rights and social and cultural distance will have a crucial impact on the long-term development of Cross-border E-commerce. Many future efforts should be focused on creating a healthy, open and inclusive international environment. We would improve step by step in political, economic, social, environmental, legal and other elements, which is the basic guarantee for the development of Cross-border E-commerce logistics and supply chain.

Finally, the cultivation of talents is urgent. Talents are the guarantee of logistics and supply chain integration. China's international logistics started late, and it is still in an elementary level. Contemporarily, China still lacks talents fully suitable for the development of international logistics enterprises. In addition, the quality of Cross-border logisticians should be high in both macroscopic vision and business details and skills. Employees who freshly graduated from logistics department in universities and institutions cannot meet the high requirements of logistics and supply chain industry. There is still an urgent need in the training and cultivation of professionals with international outlook and industrial experience, and professionals who are familiar with international economic rules, and cross-cultural development. A comprehensive development of professionals with multiple abilities will be the guarantee for the development of logistics industry. The government, enterprises and universities and other institutions should raise awareness and cooperate closely to cultivate qualified talents for Cross-border logistics.

2.4.4   Enhancement Target: Cost Reduction, Efficiency Increase and Service Betterment

"Cost reduction, efficiency increase and service betterment" has always been the target pursued by Cross-border logistics and supply chain. It is the goal of enterprises to reduce logistics costs, improve logistics transportation and distribution efficiency, and provide better services. For consumers, their internal desire is to buy quality and inexpensive goods in a convenient way and have a great shopping experience. They are just two sides of the same coin. In order to provide quality services, enterprises should strive to improve the responsiveness of logistics and supply chain, improve the ability to cope with risks, and promise the continuity and efficiency of services (Du Zhiping, 2020; Pang Yan, 2015), which is one of the core competitivenesses of Cross-border E-commerce logistics and supply chain. It is also a final standard to verify the value of international logistics and supply chain (Qi Fei, 2020).

Chapter 3　Predicaments and Risk Assessment of Cross-border E-commerce Logistics and Supply Chain

This chapter analyzes various predicaments and risks from both macro and micro perspectives based on the logistics and supply chain ecosystem. This chapter functions as a basis for the optimization scheme in Chapter 4.

3.1　Predicaments of China's Cross-border E-commerce Logistics and Supply Chain

The flows of goods and logistics lag far behind the flows of information and capital, Which has become a bottleneck in the development of Cross-border E-commerce. The reasons are that China's logistics and supply chain started relatively late, and developed with relatively backward infrastructure and management concepts (Zhao Guanghua, 2014).

3.1.1　High Cost

Cost is one of the issues that Cross-border logistics and supply chain is highly concerned about. Compared to domestic logistic delivery, Cross-border E-commerce logistics faces a long physical distance, resulting in high logistics rates. Compared to traditional foreign trade logistics, Cross-border E-commerce logistics has a fragmented demand, high transportation frequency, and more logistics sections, which also lead to high logistics rates. Among the factors that affect the cost of Cross-border E-commerce logistics, transportation cost (especially the first-leg transportation cost) takes the major part of the whole logistics price. In the final quoted price of Cross-border logistics transportation, packaging fees, labor costs, management fees, and shipping fees are high, which will squeeze the profit of Cross-border E-commerce platforms and sellers. Although the quotation price of logistics special line is lower than that of commercial express, special line is less flexible, and it is difficult to predict and control foreign markets accurately, which often results in a backlog of goods and increasing inventory costs. In addition, the coverage of the last mile delivery is less efficient, which will increase logistics distribution costs. Small-sized items are usually transported through international commercial express and international postal air mail, such as EUB(ePacket), DHL, FedEx, UPS, TNT, etc. Although timeliness can be guaranteed, freight rates remain high (Yang Zi *et al.*, 2018, Zhao Guanghua, 2014). The high freight inevitably leads to high price of products, which greatly weakens the price advantage of Chinese commodities, thereby reducing the international competitiveness of Chinese products.

3.1.2   Low Supply Chain Efficiency

The low efficiency of Cross-border logistics and supply chain is mainly reflected in two aspects: Firstly, customs clearance efficiency is not high. In some countries, the infrastructure for Cross-border commodity inspection and customs clearance is backward and procedures are complex. Also, the documents and procedures of exported goods are not complete, the quantity is underreported, and the quality of commodities is not up to a certain standard. In addition, there is insufficient understanding of relevant laws and regulations on the packaging standard, resulting in unqualified product packaging, unclear product descriptions and infringement of intellectual property rights (for example, an infringement of trademark) that seriously affect the efficiency of customs clearance. Secondly, the efficiency of transportation and distribution needs to be improved. The time cost of long-distance Cross-border transportation, especially maritime transportation, is huge, resulting in the customers' long-wait to receive their goods. The speed of Cross-border E-commerce logistics and distribution is an important factor affecting overseas buyers' purchases. Customers in Europe and the United States have high requirements for logistic timeliness. If delivery time exceeds their expectations, they would complain and even cause transaction failures. It regularly takes 5 – 10 days for China Post air mail to send parcels to neighboring Asian countries, 7 – 15 days to major European and American countries, 15 – 30 days to other countries and regions (Zhao Guanghua, 2014). Long delivery time can easily lead to a huge backlog of goods, and the backlog would cause longer delivery time, thus bringing an aggravating vicious cycle. For example, Hong Kong Post air mail is the most used package service for sellers of small transaction quantity. It has been reported that there is repeated overstocking due to excessive business volume, making it difficult to guarantee efficiency. In addition, due to the long transport distance, it takes multiple transshipments for the logistics couriers to pick up one item and finally to deliver it to the user. It is difficult to avoid damage to the package, and there are even cases of losing items. These are all manifestations of inefficient Cross-border supply chain.

3. 1. 3　Low Integration Level

There are a large number of third-party logistics enterprises in China, and their overall development level is in transition from a growing stage to functional maturity. The overall characteristics are as follows: not-so-standard company organization and small scale business scope with a wildly growing style. There are few large, functional and highly specialized third-party logistics enterprises. Most logistics companies provide functional domestic logistics services, while international logistics and fulfillment services are mainly provided in the form of regular express delivery or postal packages. There are fewer logistics companies who could offer an integrated service that can provide good domestic, international and local logistics service. Currently, the four major international commercial express companies are still the mainstream in providing services. China Postal Express and Logistics Company Limited (Express Mail Service, EMS), SF Express and other companies are trying to develop their international logistics business and still on the way to accumulate Cross-border logistics capital and experience.

3.1.4   Low Digitalization Level

Although the level of Cross-border logistics informatization and digitalization has been greatly improved, in actual operation, the organizational structure and management model of logistics enterprises are physically simple. Most logistics companies lack digital thinking in many aspects like inventory management, resulting in a certain difference between inventory prediction and actual sales, and leading to unscientific inventory cost control, especially in the operation of overseas warehouses. A precise sales forecasting is the key to control warehousing in overseas warehouses, and the level of digitalization directly affects the cost and efficiency of overseas warehouse operations. The low level of digitalization also leads to the problems of incomplete logistics information and untimely tracking in some Cross-border logistics transactions. At the same time, due to the low adoption of information technology and various information technology standards in different countries, it is difficult to effectively connect logistics information systems between logistics enterprises, resulting in delayed updates of logistics information. And it is difficult for consumers to track the transportation sections and locations of goods in a timely manner, which greatly affects the Cross-border shopping experience for customers. In summary, it is on the basis of information technology that Cross-border E-commerce logistics and supply chain can develop in a functional way. The lack of digital management concept can lead to various problems, such as backward static inventory management, poor supply chain management capabilities, inability to respond quickly and accurately to consumer demand and market changes, and inability to meet consumer tracking needs for logistics services (Pu Xinrong, 2022). The low level of digital development and inability to match the company's growth rate will lead to weak ability of risk resistance in Cross-border logistics enterprises. It would reduce logistics and supply chain resilience, and thus be unable to counter various operational risks arising from logistics and supply chain.

3.1.5   Low Integration of Overseas Warehouse Resources

Overseas warehouse is important overseas node for Cross-border E-commerce. It is a new type of logistics infrastructure. The real value of overseas warehouse lies in its comprehensive integration. In terms of logistics, it is mainly reflected in the integration of the supply chain in order to reduce logistics costs. For example, as the categories of Cross-border E-commerce gradually increased and upgraded, there are an increasing number of large and heavy commodities such as furniture, outdoor facilities and other big-sized household products. However, Cross-border E-commerce participants are mainly small- and medium-sized enterprises, making it difficult to distribute big-sized commodities through the high-cost traditional international distribution channels. Overseas warehouses have become an inevitable choice. Mainstream E-commerce platforms, such as eBay and Amazon, encourage or even require Chinese sellers to use more overseas warehouse shipping to guarantee user experience. Some logistics companies are trying to choose big mature markets to build overseas warehouses, such as XRU (Ruston Express) , which jointly builds " overseas warehouses" in Russia. Guangzhou's export logistics companies are also building their own inventory centers in the UK, the United States, Australia, Russia and Spain. However, the construction and operation costs of overseas warehouses are startlingly high, and it is mainly applicable to goods with high prices and large market sales potential. The present overseas warehouses are operated exclusively by big sellers with strong financial support. They usually don't share their own overseas warehouses with small- and medium-sized E-commerce enterprises who sell small-sized and low-value products. Therefore, most overseas warehouses are not open to small-and medium-sized enterprises at present, making it difficult to achieve the benefits of sharing economy of limited overseas warehouse resources. In addition to the above micro-level issues, macroscopically speaking, challenges of overseas warehouse are mainly manifested in the following two aspects.

3. 1. 6   Global Economic Recession Expectation

Investment in the logistics and supply chain is huge that requires the support of a steady development of Cross-border E-commerce industry. Since 2020, in the context of the global economic downturn, venture capital has been cautious in investing in Cross-border E-commerce logistics and supply chain. Moreover, the Cross-border E-commerce logistics and supply chain has a thin profit margin and requires long-term operation. An unstable global economic environment poses more risks of investment and offers low expected returns. In addition, the trend of global cooperation is segmented by regional economic integration, and the operation of RCEP (Regional Comprehensive Economic Partnership), CPTPP (Comprehensive and Progressive Agreement for Trans-Pacific Partnership), and USMCA (The United States-Mexico-Canada Agreement) hinder the role of international organizations, such as WTO (World Trade Organization). The wave of anti-globalization is neither conducive to the development of global economic integration, nor conducive to the establishment and maintenance of Cross-border E-commerce logistics and supply chain. Besides that, the news of layoffs on Cross-border E-commerce big techs, such as Amazon, eBay and AliExpress may lead the industry into a readjustment stage, and the chain of the industry will also be adjusted accordingly.

3.1.7 Increased Instability Factors in the Ecosystem

In a complex Cross-border E-commerce logistics and supply chain ecosystem, each species may face and pose certain risks and challenges, and the coordination between the micro-level enterprises and industries and the macro-level countries will always be inconsistent. In addition, many problems are apparent, such as the establishment of trust mechanisms, the protection of Intellectual Property Rights, data transmission and exchange, individual privacy protection, and the widespread application of advanced technologies, such as blockchain. It needs a long time for these to be tested by enterprises and the whole market. There still exists a need for continuous communication among countries, and the development of Cross-border E-commerce and logistics industries would be promoted step by step in the process of establishing new rules, standards, and modes.

3.2 Risk Assessment of Cross-border E-commerce Logistics and Supply Chain

In the context of Cross-border E-commerce, Cross-border logistics services involve many risks in different aspects, such as multiple logistics models, customs clearance, third-party payment platforms, and Internet information, etc. These factors may be superposed by diverse political, legal, economic, and geographical environments of multiple countries. There would be a great diversity in risks (Gao Fan, 2020). Many scholars have conducted research on the identification and evaluation of risks, which can be roughly categorized into internal risks and external risks, and which are in consistent with the micro and macro influencers of the Cross-border E-commerce logistics and supply chain ecosystem.

3. 2. 1   Research on Third-party Cross-border Logistics and Supply Chain Risks

In the process of selecting third-party Cross-border logistics, Cross-border E-commerce requires risk identification. Ju Yongmei (2020) classified its risks into internal risks and external risks, as shown in Figure 3 – 1, which were further divided into eight dimensions and covered 28 items. Internal risks mainly included strategic risks, supply risks, cooperation risks, and information risks, which were risks faced by Cross-border E-commerce industry and the process of cooperation. External risks mainly involved transportation risks, packaging and warehousing risks, environmental risks, loading and unloading risks, and customs risks, which are risks that may exist in third-party logistics enterprises. After analyzing the significance of these risks, she concluded that cooperation risk was the main risk faced by Cross-border E-commerce when selecting third-party logistics.

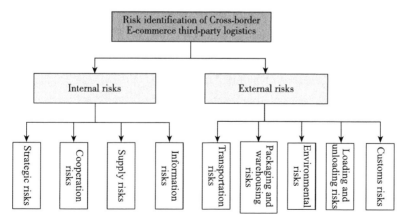

Figure 3 – 1   Internal and External Risk Identification of Cross-border E-commerce Third-party Logistics

Giuffrida *et al.* (2021) believed that there were seven types of uncertainties in Cross-border logistics processes: delivery uncertainty, customer service expectation uncertainty, compliance uncertainty, external uncertainty, inventory management uncertainty, product or parcel damage, uncertainty in demand forecasting and management. These uncertainties were risks that logistics companies must consider when conducting business operations. Enterprises should adopt appropriate strategies to conduct business based on risks.

Based on literature research, Yang Zi *et al.* (2018) divided the influencing factors of Cross-border E-commerce logistics transportation into macro and micro perspectives. The macro perspective included political, economic, social, and technological aspects, while the micro perspective included Cross-border E-commerce enterprises, third-party logistics platforms, markets, and consumers. According to the development of global Cross-border E-commerce logistics, following the principles of standardization, comparability, operability, and comprehensiveness, a three-level indicator system for evaluating the factors was established based on the hierarchical analysis method. Among the second-level indicators, the authors conducted a fuzzy hierarchical analysis from five aspects: information system construction, logistics system cost, international transportation quality, transportation entity capacity, and external environment maintenance. Their results showed that the information system construction was the most important constraint factor, and the ranking of other factors was international transportation quality, external environment maintenance, transportation entity capacity, and finally, logistics system cost. Therefore, the authors believed that the construction of logistics information system was an important aspect of Cross-border logistics and must be taken seriously. At the third-level indicators, a few specific aspects such as information platform construction, logistics technology application, international logistics law, level of third-party logistics, customs and commodity inspection, policy environment, logistics management capabilities, logistics enterprise scale operations, product market conditions, and talent cultivation constituted constraints to the development of Cross-border E-commerce logistics and supply chain. These findings also confirmed the importance of maintaining the logistics and supply chain ecosystem in Chapter 1. Therefore, the authors proposed to promote the structural upgrading of Cross-border logistics industry, strengthen policy support for logistics transportation, innovate the distribution mode of logistics enterprises, and improve the quality of Cross-border logistics services. These suggestions have also received many responses in other studies.

3. 2. 2   Case Studies

Gao Fan (2020) conducted a case study using Shenzhen WANB Express as an example to analyze the risks faced by small-and medium-sized Cross-border logistics enterprises. There are four potential risks: logistics risks, customs clearance risks, transaction risks, and Force Majeure risks, as shown in Figure 3 – 2. He also proposed preventive measures for small-and medium-sized logistics enterprises: renting or sharing overseas warehouses, improving logistics information systems, and establishing their own customs clearance companies. The author suggested

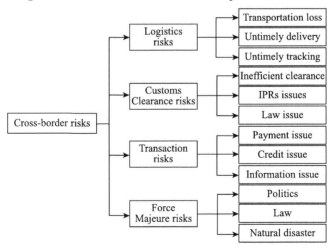

Figure 3 – 2   Cross-border Logistics Risks

using blockchain technology for Cross-border payments, and strengthening aware-ness of external risks which were enlightening to the development of small-and medium-sized logistics enterprises.

For special situations, each risk category has its own characteristics. Xie Si-xin *et al.* (2019) analyzed the main internal and external risks faced by Cross-border E-commerce logistics alliances against the background of trade frictions between China and the United States. External risks mainly included general envi-ronmental risks, economic environmental risks, and market environmental risks, while internal risks mainly included financing risks, logistics capability risks, and management and coordination ability risks. The way to address risks was to build an innovative Cross-border E-commerce smart logistics ecosystem, and carry out risk prevention and control in a trinity, that is, prediction, capability, and coordi-nation, which was an effective measure to improve the risk resistance ability of China's Cross-border E-commerce logistics alliance. Zhao Xindong (2022) ana-lyzed the logistics risks and difficulties faced by Cross-border E-commerce against the background status after the COVID-19, and believed that the current Cross-border logistics risks were mainly logistics risks with customs clearance as the core element and capital risks with inventory as the core element.

In terms of risk analysis of logistics modes, Zheng Xiaoxue *et al.* (2016) ana-lyzed the risks faced by Cross-border logistics enterprises. Taking the analysis of Cross-border E-commerce logistics modes and risk factors as a starting point, the authors used extension models to conduct simulation calculation. They divided the risk indicators faced by two types of enterprises into four levels, and conducted risk assessments on enterprises from several aspects, such as market risk, customs clearance risk and transportation risk. Based on a comprehensive analysis of the four main models of Cross-border logistics—postal logistics, international commer-cial express, international logistics special lines, and overseas warehouses, Zhang Duo *et al.* (2019) used a fuzzy comprehensive evaluation method to assess and predict the risks of Cross-border E-commerce logistics modes. Their results showed that there were significant differences in the impact of seven risks, and it was necessary to prevent and control logistics risks. Risk prevention and control measures should be focusd on improving the logistics system, jointly building logistics alliances, improving information technology, improving management mechanisms, and preventing and controlling exchange rate risk.

Logistics alliance is the trend of Cross-border E-commerce logistics and supply chain development. Tian Qing *et al.* (2021) studied the risks existing in the operation of the current logistics alliance model. They included market change risks, transportation security risks, financing risks, logistics capability risks and alliance management risks. Basically, they can be classified into two categories: logistics risks and supply chain operational risks. Du Zhiping and Gong Xianglin (2018) conducted a research on logistics operational risk in Cross-border logistics alliances. Starting from the characteristics of Cross-border logistics, such as large spatial span, complex logistics network, and multiple node changes, they proposed external mechanisms or management methods to reduce risks.

Liu Yongsheng *et al.* (2012) analyzed enterprise logistics risks and proposed that enterprises faced seven risk factors, including environmental risks, market risks, supply logistics risks, production logistics risks, sales logistics risks, returned logistics risks, and overall logistics risks. On this basis, they proposed to design a logistics early warning risk indicator system based on enterprise operation processes. They constructed and analyzed the system based on enterprise operation process. In general, there are still some aspects to be improved in the existing research. The logistics risks faced by Cross-border logistics alliances can be prevented in advance by establishing a logistics risk early warning mechanism system, thereby reducing the cost increase caused by risks. However, the prevention and avoidance of logistics risks is dependent on the smooth operation efficiency of the logistics alliance chain. The cooperation risk was the main risk faced by Cross-border logistics alliances (Du Zhiping, 2018). He also proposed that the cooperation risk determined the stable and normal operation of logistics alliances. Effective risk management can better enhance the stability of Cross-border logistics alliances by establishing a reasonable benefit allocation mechanism and strengthening the value creation mechanism.

Jiang Xu and Jiang Feifei (2015) analyzed the transaction cost theory and believed that alliances had external uncertainties, including environmental uncertainty and partner behavior uncertainty. Research showed that effective management of alliance risk by enterprices can improve the satisfaction of alliance cooperation performance. Li Shiping *et al.* (2014) found that implementing a sharing mechanism can maximize the benefits of alliance members through research on an aviation alliance formed by two airlines. Zhou Min and Huang Fuhua (2013), starting from the operational characteristics of logistics alliances, analyzed the behavior patterns of each member of logistics alliances according to game theory, discussed the cooperation risk sharing scheme, as well as the rationality and stability of the scheme, and proposed establishing a risk public welfare fund system to solve the problem of risk sharing in Cross-border logistics alliances.

In summary, Cross-border logistics risks are mainly reflected in Figure 3 – 3.

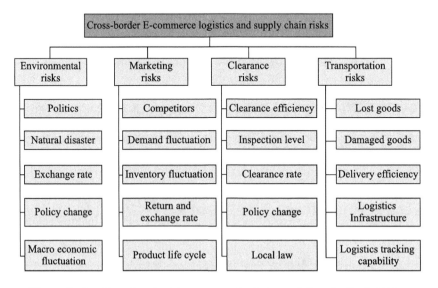

Figure 3 – 3   Cross-border E-commerce Logistics and Supply Chain Risks

3. 3   Risk Assessment of Overseas Warehouse

According to present studies, the main risks faced by China's overseas warehouse management are operational risks and decision-making risks. As a new logistics mode, overseas warehouse plays a significant role in solving many practical operational risks faced by China's current export trade, such as poor timeliness, low after-sales efficiency, high logistics costs, and inaccurate inventory, etc. For the purpose of optimization, domestic and foreign scholars have conducted extensive research on the risks faced by overseas warehouse operations from different perspectives. Cao Qian and Jiang Jing (2022) believed that the main risks faced by overseas warehouse enterprises were legal and policy risks, market risks, management risks and cost risks. Zhou Guanglan and Fan Zhiying (2021) used system dynamics modeling to explore the impact of overseas warehouse services on Cross-border E-commerce export transactions. Through sensitivity analysis, they believed that the biggest barrier to overseas warehouse services was customs clearance risk. Therefore, Cross-border logistics enterprises may take customs clearance into first consideration when allocating investment in various businesses of overseas warehouses. Guo Wenqiang and Wang Yanbo (2022) analyzed three overseas warehouse types: FBA, self-built overseas warehouse and third-party overseas warehouse. They believed that the three were suitable for different enterprises and different developmental stages. Therefore, different enterprises should select suitable overseas warehouses types based on their own characteristics. Fang Si (2020) proposed that the selection of overseas warehouse types is directly related to the risk level of operating efficiency. Therefore, an overseas warehouse selection strategy should be based on the overall consideration of the three factors: the personel (human resources), categories (products) and countries (places). It is recommended that enterprises should determine their appropriate overseas warehouse type based on their own development situation, product type, and destination. Overseas warehouse is a capital-intensive and technology-intensive industry in nature that requires a large amount of capital and human resource investment. However, capital issue and talent shortage are currently the issues faced by most Cross-border E-commerce logistics enterprises. In response, Tao Zheng (2021) proposed that enterprises can rely on industrial clusters to establish Cross-border logistics alliances, and jointly build overseas warehouses through agreements, joint ventures, and equity investments. Moreover, enterprises should establish overseas warehouse risk warning mechanisms to resist overseas warehouse predicaments. Quan Yin (2020) proposed a method of establishing shared overseas warehouses based on the sharing economy to share overseas warehouse resources and information by establishing a comprehensive service platform.

The emergence of overseas warehouses has greatly promoted the further development of Cross-border E-commerce, but the risks appeared in operation are also numerous compared with those in domestic warehouses. The control and counter measures for overseas warehouse risks will be discussed in detail in Chapter 5.

3. 4　Macro-Level Risk Assessment

In addition to the analysis and evaluation of Cross-border logistics risks at the micro-level, many scholars have also focused on the macro-level issues that affect the development of Cross-border logistics. However, compared to the micro-level research, there are relatively few studies focusing on the macro environment of Cross-border E-commerce in China.

Firstly, in terms of Cross-border logistics and supply chain policies, the research on the macro environment based on PEST (Political, Economic, Social and

Technological) theory is relatively mature. Guo Yan *et al.* (2020) used the PEST analysis model to analyze the macro competitive environment of China's Cross-border E-commerce from four aspects: politics, economy, society, and technology. The promulgation of macro policies on Cross-border logistics and supply chain in China has undergone two stages, namely, the central legislative stage since 2013 and the regional legislative stage in various provinces and cities. In terms of policy content, it focused on collecting the needs of enterprises. It was the government that should establish Cross-border E-commerce systematic standards that were compatible with digital E-commerce. The study suggested that more platforms should be built to create ways for small- and medium-sized enterprises to obtain effective information. The government should also ensure that policies conform to local regional development characteristics and promote precise trade policies that conform to local characteristics.

Xiong Li and Ye Kaiwen (2020) proposed a Cross-border E-commerce ecosystem from a policy perspective. They analyzed the correlation between Cross-border E-commerce ecological development and Cross-border E-commerce policies, and proposed an "ecosystem policy combination" analysis framework, as shown in Figure 3 − 4. The policy portfolio was classified into four categories: environment-side policies (accounting for 74.51%), supply-side policies (accounting for 14.52%), demand-side policies (accounting for 2.9%), and evaluation-side policies (accounting for 8.06%). The four types of policies cooperated with each other and promoted the healthy development of Cross-border E-commerce ecosystem through the joint action of "construction—push—pull—evaluation". Among the policies at the central government level, environment-side policies were used the most, followed by supply-side policies and evaluation-side policies. Demand-side policies were in serious shortage situation. The study believed that the impact of existing policies on the Cross-border E-commerce ecosystem had gone deep into the fields of payment, taxation, supervision, logistics, informationization, etc. But there was still a shortage in the aspects of professionals and logisticians, and the content of intellectual property protection, etc. In the serious absence of demand-side policies, it was necessary to strengthen the function of guidance at the central government's policy in terms of international cooperation, tax policies, expansion of exports and domestic demand, to stimulate consumer demand. In addition, macroeconomic policies were not sufficiently integrated into the entire Cross-border logistics ecosystem, and the role of regulation to support it had not yet been formed.

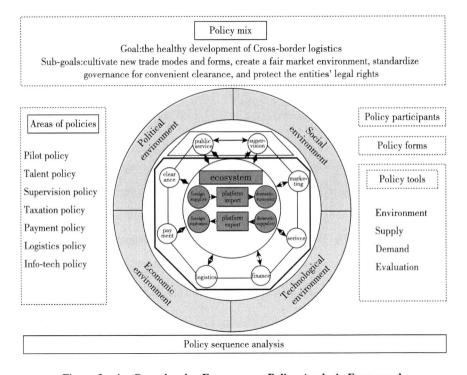

Figure 3 – 4   Cross-border E-commerce Policy Analysis Framework

Secondly, in terms of institutional distance and cultural distance, most studies focused on differences in institutional environments, such as economy, politics, law and culture differences among countries. Scholars have conducted research on how to shorten and bridge institutional distance. Some scholars also incorporated cultural distance into the refinement of institutional distance, believing that the cultural distance represented by cultural differences was also one of the factors that cause institutional distance. Other scholars added policy factors to the institutional distance. Estrin *et al.* (2009) distinguished formal and informal institutional distances, the former including legal provisions and business practices, and the latter including cultural practices, values and social beliefs. Institutional distance, cultural distance, and geographical distance were considered obstacles to the development of Cross-border E-commerce and Cross-border logistics and supply chain.

Li Yuanxu and Luo Jia (2017) used cultural distance and institutional distance theory to analyze risks in Cross-border E-commerce from a consumer perspective. Institutional distance includes two aspects, namely economic system and legal system. The economic system was measured by the "Economic Freedom Index" published by the Heritage Foundation, *the Wall Street Times*, and the Fraser Institute of Canada. The legal system was measured by "Worldwide Governance Indicators" (WGI). Based on the obtained data on the economic and legal systems of various countries, the institutional distance among countries was constructed. Borrowing the risk classification of western scholars for reference, they used five dimensions to measure the perceived risk by consumers: (1) Seller's risk. It referred to the behavior of E-commerce sellers that harmed the interests of customers in pursuit of maximum benefits. (2) Product risk. It referred to consumers' concerns that a product cannot meet the expected needs in terms of quality and performance. (3) Economic risk. It referred to the fear that online shopping may cause financial losses or additional costs. (4) Delivery risk. It referred to the fear related to product damage or loss due to delivery. (5) The risk of misuse of personal information. It referred to the fear that personal information might be stolen or misused. Based on the five dimensions, measurement items were prepared. They used four cultural dimensions, namely power distance, individualism, uncertainty avoidance, and masculinity to measure cultural distance. The results of research showed that cultural distance had a significant impact on Cross-border E-commerce risks in the five dimensions, and economic system distance significantly affected the seller's risk, economic risk and personal information abuse risk of customers. In contrast, legal system distance had no impact on product risk, but excessive legal distance can affect the other four risks. Differences in economic systems had an impact on not only Cross-border E-commerce, but also the export competitiveness of service trade (Song Jinrui and Cui Riming, 2021). Therefore, the optimization from the perspective of institutional distance and cultural distance was also an inevitable choice for Cross-border logistics and supply chain optimization.

Chapter 4　Optimization of Cross-border E-commerce Logistics and Supply Chain

Based on the Cross-border E-commerce ecosystem, this chapter focuses on the optimization of Cross-border logistics and supply chain to promote the long-term, healthy and sustainable development of Cross-border E-commerce.

The ecosystem of the Cross-border logistics and supply chain is both intricate and complex, spanning across different countries, connecting various industries, integrating multiple transportation modes. Even the slightest error in any point might lead to aggregated transaction cost or reduced efficiency. Therefore, the optimization of Cross-border logistics and supply chain is a long-term and internal imperative.

4. 1　Macro-level Optimization

The Cross-border E-commerce logistics ecosystem is shaped by the external environment. The previous chapter of this book analyzed the macro-risks in the Cross-border E-commerce logistics and supply chain. On the basis of this analysis, this chapter will present optimization plans for the macro environment of

Cross-border logistics. The plan is developed under the context of the digital economy. Therefore, the optimization of the macro environment is mainly built on the principle of shortening trade, digital and institutional distances.

In order to achieve this goal, it is necessary to take into account various factors, such as trade policies, digital infrastructure, and consumer behavior patterns. The optimization of the macro environment must also address various challenges, in fields of Cross-border regulations, digitalization and standardization, low-carbon and green supply chain, etc.

By improving the macro environment, Cross-border E-commerce logistics will become more efficient, flexible and secure, thereby supporting the sustainable development of the industry. Moreover, this will also drive innovation and facilitate the integration of digital and traditional businesses to create a more favorable environment for Cross-border trade.

4.1.1 Optimization Principle

4.1.1.1 Shorten Trade Distance

Geographical distance, institutional distance, and cultural distance are the three components that make up trade distance, which hinders the growth of Cross-border E-commerce. Tang Hongtao and Zhu Mengqi (2021) referred to these three factors as trade costs. The optimization of Cross-border logistics aims to reduce costs and increase efficiency, thus lowering the cost of Cross-border logistics. Internet technology has helped Cross-border E-commerce enterprises to cross geographical distance in a practical sense. It is widely acknowledged that the use of E-commerce has reduced the cost of trade-related geographical distance. Cultural differences cannot be eliminated easily, and it requires frequent and in-depth communication to bridge cultural distance. The optimization policies, if designed to fit for Cross-border E-commerce circumstances, can surely shorten the cultural distance. For example, Cross-border E-commerce platform provides multilingual service support, which can help reduce communication costs, improve transaction efficiency, and shorten cultural distance.

4. 1. 1. 2   Shorten Institutional Distance

Institutional distance, also considered as a component of trade distance, will be discussed separately in this section. Shortening institutional distance is not an easy task, especially under the current global economic landscape, where Cross-border E-commerce is facing trade protectionism, anti-globalization trend, and trade friction. All of these are the very embodiment of institutional distance. As to the institutional distance in Cross-border E-commerce, Tang Hongtao and Zhu Mengqi (2021) focused their research on the economic aspect. In their opinion, shortening institutional distance meant the shortening of economic institutional distance. Therefore, the development of Cross-border E-commerce and logistics is reciprocally intertwined with the shortening of institutional distance. The promotion of intergovernmental cooperation, and the consistency in business practice and transaction process are crucial in weakening institutional gap of Cross-border E-commerce.

The economic institution consists of different policies in various countries and regions concerning international economic rules, intellectual property protection, personal privacy protection and data transmission. The differences in policies inevitably limit the smooth operation of Cross-border E-commerce and logistics. The key to reduce the institutional distance is to narrow the gap with target countries and to realize the connection, docking, integrating and revising in the economic system. The institutional system of China's Cross-border E-commerce and logistics is still in its early stage. Due to the short developing period, the legal system is not fully formed. Some domestic rules don't agree with international rules seamlessly. Some are even in conflict with international rules. And there is a lack of relevant rules and regulations in some aspects. All in all, the law and regulation system is under-developed in China. Therefore, from the perspective of shortening institutional distance, the following two points should be focused on. Firstly, we should work hard to shorten the distance of both economic institution and legal institution with developed countries to enhance Chinese product recognition in these markets. These would help a lot to lower the potential risks and improve the transaction rate with consumers in these countries. Secondly, our government should work on achieving coordination, connection, convergence, and adjustment of domestic and international policies to actively reduce trade friction and barrier. By promoting the coordination of industrial, trade and competition policies, we can establish a fairer global market environment and a better integration with the international market (Pu Xinrong, 2022).

4. 1. 1. 3   Shorten Digital Distance

As the significance of digital technology in Cross-border E-commerce grows, the concept of "digital distance" has emerged. Digital distance refers to the widening gap in digital technology development among countries, regions and enterprises due to the differences in the level of information infrastructure and network technology. This uneven development leads to problems such as inefficient global supply chain information flow, lack of data sharing, and poor coordination. These digital barriers, in turn, result in reduced efficiency, increased cost, and a low customer experience in the logistics process. Yang Jijun *et al.* (2022) described digital distance as the "digital gap", which encompassed the following three aspects: the "access gap", which was a result of uneven development of digital infrastructure and Internet access; the "implementation gap", which refers to the gap in mastering digital knowledge and implementation of digital technology; and the "capacity gap", which refers to the ability of access to data resources and the creation of data wealth. The word "gap" highlights the severity of digital distance, and it is challenging to overcome in a short time. Under the synergistic push of Matthew effect in digital supply chain, the privileged countries will become stronger, while the underprivileged become weaker.

The digital infrastructure of developing countries is relatively backward, and there is not an adequate context for its development. These lead to a limited participation in the global industrial and supply chain division of labor. Meanwhile, big digital economies have an advantage in digital access, which can trigger a positive feedback mechanism in the digital industrial chain and make the strong even stronger. Currently, 80% of global data and core technology are controlled by developed countries, which seriously restricts the progress of the digital economy in developing countries.

4.1.2　Optimization Strategy

To optimize Cross-border E-commerce, it's important to take into consideration the following six major factors that make up the Cross-border E-commerce logistics and supply chain ecosystem, namely political, economic, social, technological, environmental and legal. Firstly, the government should work on improving political and economic cooperation through increased communication, which requires a mutual understanding of various cultures. Hence, enhancing cultural identification could lay a solid foundation for further economic cooperation. Secondly, the government should support Cross-border platforms by promoting the digitalization of Cross-border platforms and the standardization of their operations. These would provide a good business environment for platform's digital transformation. Lastly, guided by the goal of carbon peaking and carbon neutrality, the government and businesses should work together to ensure a green and low-carbon development of the Cross-border supply chain. These macro-optimization policies will help to integrate and streamline the Cross-border E-commerce logistics and supply chain and to realize a healthy growth of Cross-border E-commerce.

4.1.2.1　Increase Social Culture Identification

In addition to providing policy support for Cross-border E-commerce enterprises, the government should also engage in cultural dissemination on a global scale. This involves integrating Chinese culture into the world culture, enhancing its international recognition while preserving its distinctive features. On the basis of cultural communication, further steps can be taken to facilitate trade communication and strengthen cooperation with other countries. A friendly image of China in international commerce communication should be built to attract more countries to cooperate with us. It helps to gain the trust of overseas users in Chinese products (Li Yuanxu and Luo Jia, 2017).

4.1.2.2　Promote Digital Empowerment

The trend of Cross-border logistics is the digital-empowered logistic infrastructure. As the pipeline for information, it plays a crucial role in supporting high-quality Cross-border logistics. It's crucial to establish a sound legal framework for the digital economy. This includes strengthening the governance of the digital economy and guiding platform businesses to operate under legal framework. Additionally, it is important to maintain a fair and orderly market competition environment and ensure policy-making and alignment supported by big data.

4.1.2.3　Develop Low-Carbon Logistics and Supply Chain

Under the carbon peaking and carbon neutrality goals, China's foreign trade faces significant challenges. Countries around the world also set their own dual-carbon goals. These dual-carbon goals, both domestic and international, will impose a major impact on the development of China's Cross-border E-commerce. Chinese government and enterprises need to respond quickly to these challenges by transitioning the structures of foreign trade and logistics and supply chain. Besides that, they are facing pressures from developed countries, such as carbon barriers, carbon tariffs, and complex trade policies. The objective of fulfilling China's carbon reduction obligations, implementing low-carbon economic development, and driving the low-carbon development of Cross-border E-commerce and logistics (Wang Xiaoyu *et al.* ,2021) poses significant challenges to our country's environmental protection concepts, practices, policies and regulations. For instance, fast fashion Cross-border E-commerce company SheIn has achieved great success due to its high-quality logistics and supply chain, but it is also under immense pressure from social and environmental responsibilities. [1] Environmental concern has become the most criticized aspect of the fast fashion industry.

4. 1. 2. 4 Improve Laws and Regulations

To promote the development of the Cross-border E-commerce, Chinese government has implemented supportive policies, such as the *Guiding Opinions on Promoting the Healthy and Rapid Development of Cross-border E-commerce* issued by the State Council in 2015 and the *Fourteenth Five-Year Plan Modern Logistics Development Plan* issued in 2022, which have played an instrumental role in promoting the development of China's Cross-border E-commerce at the policy level. Li Yifan and Chen Juan (2022) pointed out three key areas for standardizing the domestic Cross-border logistics industry. Firstly, improving industry standards will help to create a good port shipping logistics environment. Secondly, cracking down on illegal practices like monopoly, speculative reselling, and malicious shipment booking will help to stabilize shipping costs. Thirdly, promoting standardized management of the domestic section, and fostering effective communication and collaboration among all local governments and regulatory authorities will help to strengthen government supervision. Supplemented by tax preferential policies or government financial subsidies and other relevant policy preferences, the three

---

[1] https://baijiahao. baidu. com/s? id = 1738958743073736548&wfr = spider&for = pc, 24 – 1 – 2023.

policy orientations aim to form the blueprint of the Cross-border E-commerce. For example, in response to the challenges posed by the pandemic, government departments stipulated a few rules and guidelines. Supportive policies for small- and medium-sized enterprises helped them strengthen their anti-risk ability and are good to promote future high-quality growth for the Cross-border E-commerce industry.

The current framework of laws and regulations for Cross-border E-commerce in China is still incomplete, and China's participation in international E-commerce rules is limited. Currently, only a few bilateral and regional trade agreements have special sections dedicated to E-commerce. With the rapid development of the digital economy, China's Cross-border E-commerce rules should focus on intangible digital products and services trade, and relevant Intellectual Property Rights and tax rules should be adjusted accordingly. Besides, the relationship between Cross-border E-commerce trade and network security needs to be redefined. Although the rules of Cross-border E-commerce and digital trade in Europe and the United States are relatively mature, China still needs to formulate its own rules in line with Chinese conditions. On the basis of borrowing foreign experiences, China should continuously improve Cross-border E-commerce logistics and supply chain rules through top-level design, domestic rule making, international rule participation, bilateral and regional negotiation practices (Chen Zhijuan, 2021).

In conclusion, on a macro level, the modern commerce logistics system in China has begun to develop and form its scale under the guidance of policy dividends, which lays a foundation for future development. The government, while introducing supportive policies, needs to further study the actual operating practices of enterprises, pay more attention to the actual problems and solve the actual operating difficulties of enterprises.

4. 2   Micro-level Optimization

The Cross-border E-commerce logistics and supply chain is a complex system, involving not only the complexity of the macro environment mentioned above but also other aspects such as Cross-border E-commerce platforms, Cross-border logistics platforms, domestic supply chain platforms, and Cross-border payment systems. It encompasses various Cross-border E-commerce entities including suppliers, manufacturers, distributors, retailers and consumers. In general, the overall ability of Cross-border logistics and supply chain companies is primarily reflected in three dimensions: information capability, logistics capability and financial capability, which serve as three pillars of the logistics industry. From these three points of view, this part will discuss how to improve the information capability of Cross-border logistics through the digital optimization scheme, how to improve the logistics and financial capability through the alliance optimization scheme. Based on these conceptions, this part will further put forward the optimization scheme of China's Cross-border E-commerce logistics development model, centering around two essential themes of the digital economy and logistics alliance.

4. 2. 1   Digitalization of Cross-border Logistics and Supply Chain

The information capability of Cross-border logistics businesses is intricately linked to the digital economy. For those businesses, the information capability needs to be continuously improved. The upgraded digital capability, in turn, enhances the resilience and flexibility of the Cross-border E-commerce supply chain, thereby improving its overall risk resistance capability.

Digital economy is a series of economic activities that employ digital knowledge and information as key production factors, modern information networks as important channels, and communication technology as an important driving force for efficiency improvement and optimization of the economic structure. The development of the digital economy is of great significance. It is a strategic choice to the new opportunities of the next round of technological revolution and industrial transformation, and that we should make use of the magnifying, superimposing, and multiplicative effects of digital technology on economic development. The development scale of China's digital economy ranks at the forefront of the world, and industrial-level digitalization is an important feature of the digital economy. On March 28, 2022, China Center for International Economic Exchanges released a report entitled *Digital Platforms Help SMEs Participate in Global Supply Chain Competition*, stating that the era of digitalized international supply chain is accelerating. Currently, digital platforms use new-generation digital intelligence technologies, such as big data, cloud computing, and virtual reality to integrate data from all links of the foreign trade supply chain. There forms a new iteration of supply chain and value chain system in a broader scope, supported by new business modes, big data, network sharing, and intelligent cooperation. Chapter 3 examines the risk identification and evaluation of different logistics modes in Cross-border logistics. The higher-level risks of Cross-border logistics are mainly transportation risks, customs clearance risks and stability risks. Digitalized supply chain will help to reduce these three major risks.

4.2.1.1　Digital-empowered Supply Chain Risk Control

As new-generation digital technologies of big data, cloud computing, and artificial intelligence penetrate deeper, the global supply chain is becoming increasingly digitalized, intelligent and network-supported. Leveraging big data as the core for predicting, evaluating, and generating supply chain solutions, Cross-border supply chains are being made more resilient and flexible to respond to risks associated with Cross-border transportation, customs clearance and market conditions. It is shown in the following three aspects.

Firstly, digital technology empowers the supply chain to cope with transportation risks. Digital technology directly connects the supply side and the demand side through the platform by reducing intermediatories to make the supply chain flatter and to improve its overall smooth operation. Additionally, digital technology improves the division of labor in the supply chain and reduces cost. In the context of Cross-border E-commerce, this technology reshapes the division of labor through cost-saving and export value-added effects, promoting functional complementarity and synergy within the supply chain. Specifically speaking, digital technology permeates into every link in the industrial chain and supply chain, from production to circulation to the end-consumer. This leads to efficient and accurate matching of goods, people, money, roads, warehouses, vehicles and other elements (Yang Jijun *et al.*, 2022). By collecting discrete data scattered throughout the supply chain, digital technology assists logistics enterprises in processing big data and dynamically optimizing the supply chain network links. It also helps enterprises effectively develop channels for big data applications (Ma Shuzhong and Guo Jiwen, 2020). The adoption of digital technology not only lowers transaction cost but also predicts transportation risks in advance and therefore improves the anti-risk resilience of the supply chain. The above mentioned professional division of labor and the flattened and digitalized of processes are all signs of how digital technology empowers Cross-border E-commerce supply chain. It improves the resilience of the supply chain.

Secondly, digital technology empowers the supply chain to deal with customs clearance risks. Customs clearance is a supportive species in the Cross-border E-commerce ecosystem, playing a role in connecting all the links in the ecosystem. Platforms built on digital technology can realize various functions, such as customs declaration and inspection, export clearance, tax settlement, which are managed and constructed by customs, governments and related enterprises to achieve unified information exchange and transmission. The digital technology-powered paperless customs clearance simplifies procedures and reduces risks. Is a crucial step to improve efficiency.

Thirdly, digital technology strengthens the stability of the global supply chain. As the name suggests, the supply chain consists of interconnected businesses. Any one of these businesses that stops functioning because of external disruptions can affect the entire chain. In recent years, delays and disruptions in the supply chain have become common due to the COVID-19. The digital technology-powered Cross-border supply chain can better realize the flexibility of the supply chain, enhance its resilience, and form a dynamic supply chain model of "supply chain—blue print—policy making" (Yang Jijun *et al.* ,2022). The digital supply chain allows flexible transition from offline to online. When the offline supply chain is impacted, the digital supply chain can quickly shift the offline demand to online demand, thereby increasing the flexibility and stability of the global supply chain.

4.2.1.2　Digital Optimization Strategy of Logistics and Supply Chain

Digital technology enables the low-cost and efficient operation of China's Cross-border supply chain. Increasing the digitalization level of the Cross-border E-commerce logistics industry is an inevitable choice to break industry bottlenecks. It helps to achieve supply chain cost reduction and efficiency enhancement. It is also the foundation for creating a smart logistics system that integrates trunk line transportation, storage service, delivery service, after-sales service, sales forecasting, and inventory management (Li Yifan and Chen Juan,2022). With the support of digital technology, all parts of the entire supply chain work together to achieve the optimized value chain.

Firstly, standardize the process of Cross-border logistics and supply chain.

The digitalization of Cross-border logistics is based on the standardization of logistics processes. Taking the timeliness of Cross-border logistics as an example, since it involves multiple entities, Cross-border logistics system needs a clear standard for the timely operation of each link to smooth the whole process. In addition to the standardization of each link, the standardization of identifier (signs, labels, tags. etc.) and the standardization of processes are also key factors to Cross-border logistics digitalization and integration. For example, when a Cross-border parcel is sent from domestic to overseas, different parties are involved in each link of Cross-border logistics. Therefore, one package needs to be labeled with at least 7 to 8 tags. If these tags cannot be identified accurately, this Cross-border transaction is very likely to fail.

Secondly, take the advantages of platform integration synergy.

Guided by the integration concept, the comprehensive platform should leverage integrated synergy to significantly lower the cost and risk associated with Cross-border logistics transportation, and ultimately enhance logistics efficiency. Integration is a key direction for the sustainable development of logistics and supply chain.

When a comprehensive logistics service platform is built, it can evaluate orders, predict the logistics resources needed, integrate logistics supply data from logistics companies. Adopting the concept of sharing economy, a comprehensive logistics service platform connects information between the supply side and demand side to take advantage of the joint information in both directions. The platform provides sellers with consolidated logistics solutions such as container-sharing to reduce Cross-border logistics transportation costs and improve transportation efficiency. The information-sharing reduces the container vacancy rate, improves its intensification and provides a low-cost transportation solution for Cross-border logistics. Therefore, logistics platform companies need to enhance their overall systematization and information construction to collect, analyze and conclude data and convert the physical movement of goods into the flow of real-time electronic information. It helps to achieve a seamless matching and integration of "goods-capacity-information". To make this type of operation possible, the comprehensive platform must realize a high level information transparency. Information transparency mainly means price transparency on the platform, where the logistics companies and Cross-border sellers are connected, allowing users to pose an inquiry on the platform for a price reference. Generally speaking, this kind of platform is more like the "Ctrip" in the field of Cross-border logistics.

In addition, to enhance customer experience and build trust, the logistics information system of the platform should also focus on visualization. This means providing real-time and traceable cargo information to both sellers and customers, promptly reporting and addressing any transportation issues, reducing transportation time, ensuring cargo safety and thus improving customers' trust and satisfaction. The core of visualization lies in achieving logistics tracking and visualizing all nodes in the entire chain; therefore, it makes the illegal container transportation impossible.

Finally, refine the supply chain process with technology.

Cross-border logistics is a testing ground for advanced technology and logistic facilities. For instance, the application of cutting-edge technologies like AI (Artificial Intelligence) can help explore the smart distribution and fulfillment model, which can lead to a substantial reduction in logistics costs, minimize market risks, and increase the efficiency of the supply chain.

Currently, the Cross-border E-commerce platform utilizes advanced technologies, such as AI, blockchain and RFID (Radio Frequency Identification), to integrate data from various product and service providers in the logistics chain. This integration establishes a digital operation system that effectively manages logistics data. For example, the "YQN" platform (https://www. yunquna. com/) currently uses AI, NLP (Natural Language Processing), knowledge graphs, RPA (Robotic Process Automation), and other algorithmic capabilities to improve industry performance efficiency. It can also provide a query system offering information of port area, container cargo, shipping date, trailer positioning, ship plan, ship positioning, HS Code, trailer cost, interior loading cost, customs declaration cost, marine insurance cost, etc[①]. Cross-border E-commerce platforms should actively advance the development and implementation of drone delivery, intelligent express cabinets, and urban logistics integrated platforms to ensure promotion of "last mile" delivery, and therefore guarantee an innovative model of intelligent logistics delivery for overseas markets. Apart from technological applications in the first-leg transportation and last mile delivery, Cross-border E-commerce companies should apply digital technology to achieve network-powered, intelligent and precise information system. At the same time, the companies should also ensure the real-time synchronization with front-end sales as the guiding information for the logistics system. Logistics firms must have an in-depth understanding of the economic climate, promotion schedules, and sales trends of the destination country, utilizing smart logistics information systems to predict the market change, accurately forecast inventory levels and adjust replenishment accordingly, so as to avoid either shortage or hoarding.

Both traditional logistics and Cross-border logistics are a process of continuous integration. The integration of Cross-border logistics relies on the standardized links, comprehensive logistics platforms, and advanced technology to achieve a unified whole.

4.2.2   Integration of Cross-border Logistics and Supply Chain

As seen from the risk assessment and discussion of the Cross-border logistics alliance in Chapter 3, the Cross-border E-commerce logistics service resources are dispersed, the degree of market concentration is low, the resource sharing level is low, and the high-end services and value-added capacity are weak, all of which pose significant barriers to the growth of Cross-border E-commerce in China. To

---

① https://baijiahao. baidu. com/s? id = 1714940607259323575&wfr = spider&for = pc, 23 - 3 - 2023.

change this situation, it is necessary to integrate resources from all parties, complement each other's strengths, and form a new organizational operating model for a global logistics network that improves the overall service performance of Cross-border E-commerce logistics. This is known as a logistics alliance. The logistics alliance builds a good way to improve the overall service performance of Cross-border E-commerce logistics. Building a Cross-border logistics alliance is a pressing task for the further development of China's logistics industry.

4. 2. 2. 1 Logistics Alliance

Logistics alliance is a logistics partnership formed among enterprises, which aims to help member logistics companies achieve synergies. It is characterized by mutual trust, shared risks, and shared benefits (Tian Yu and Zhu Daoli, 2000; Du Zhiping, 2020). This alliance involves the organized market transactions conducted by all parties based on a strategic cooperation framework. On the one hand, it benefits its members by reducing the relevant costs in Cross-border E-commerce transactions; on the other hand, it is conducive to improving the ability of all parties to respond to environmental uncertainties, thus lowering operational risks (Li Xudong et al. ,2017). Representing a new iteration of Cross-border E-commerce logistics, the logistics alliance is usually established and operated around the core enterprises of a country.

4. 2. 2. 2 Developmental Stages of China's Cross-border Logistics Alliance

Li Xudong et al. (2017) summarized Cross-border E-commerce logistics alliance into three types, which is, the three stages of the development of the concept. The first stage is theprimary stage when the logistics alliance is dominated by large 3PL enterprises. Integrating other 3PL enterprises, the well-developed 3PL enterprises transform themselves into 4PL and provide integrated logistics services to their customers. The second stage is the intermediate stage when the alliance is dominated by mature 4PL enterprises or large Cross-border E-commerce platforms. The leading enterprises establish a comprehensive platform, providing all-round platform services, such as procurement, warehousing, transportation, customs clearance, packaging, distribution, after-sales service, etc. The platform works to integrate resources from various links of the Cross-border E-commerce supply chain and provide full-process services for the entire chain. The third stage is the advanced stage when the logistics alliance is dominated by global 4PL groups. This Cross-border alliance goes beyond the physical boundaries of a single industry, enabling cross-industry collaboration. It integrates Cross-border E-commerce supply chains globally, while establishing a fair mechanism for interest distribution among alliance members, resulting in mutual benefits and a win-win scenario. Furthermore, it elevates the efficiency and service level of Cross-border E-commerce logistics, and effectively reduces comprehensive logistics costs. This represents the pinnacle of Cross-border logistics alliances.

Currently, China's Cross-border logistics alliance is in its second stage. Alibaba, for example, as a core enterprise, has built a comprehensive Cross-border logistics platform by integrating various Cross-border E-commerce supply chain resources and providing customers with one-stop Cross-border E-commerce services. At this stage, Alibaba is striving to develop the alliance into the third stage. However, due to the unique national circumstances, China has established a government-led Cross-border E-commerce 4PL alliance mechanism. This mechanism is mainly deployed in Cross-border E-commerce pilot cities. The government takes the lead in building a special platform in the free trade zone, serving as the core species of the Cross-border logistics ecosystem. To build an international logistics hub, the government built Cross-border E-commerce industrial parks first by bringing together critical and supportive species of the ecosystem, including institutions of customs inspection, finance, consulting, and even peripheral species businesses. All of the species work together to form a logistics alliance ecosystem that integrates Cross-border E-commerce supply chain services.

From the above discussion on the development stages of Cross-border logistics alliance, it can be seen that the Cross-border logistics alliance is at the core of the ecosystem. The alliance prioritizes core enterprises and fosters an inclusive supply chain ecosystem that provides essential support services to participants in the logistics and supply chain. Through collaboration, participants offer tailored high-end logistics services to customers, as shown in Figure 4 − 1 (Li Xudong *et al.* ,2017).

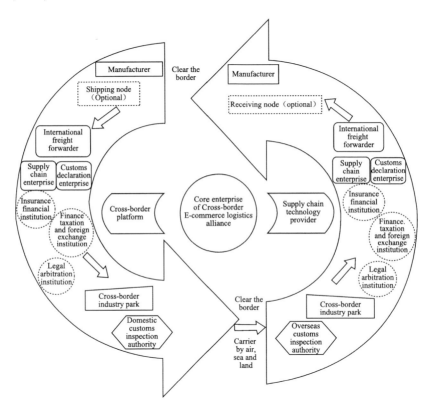

**Figure 4 – 1　Organizational Mechanism of Cross-border E-commerce
Logistics Alliance Based on 4PL**

The Cross-border logistics alliance, which is at the core of the Cross-border logistics ecosystem, plays a critical role in achieving cost-saving, efficiency-enhancing, and synergistic development of the Cross-border logistics system. As a cluster of businesses, the alliance leverages the theory of collaborative synergy to achieve better cooperative performance. The alliance helps to achieve economies of scale and ultimately, cost reduction and efficiency enhancement.

From the perspective of internal environment of an enterprise, the advantages of logistics alliance are as follows:

(1) The formation of logistics alliances promotes greater specialization in internal division of labor and enhances cooperation based on refined labor division. Similar to the theory of comparative advantage in international trade, labor division and cooperation can increase the utilization rate of resources, reduce waste, and ultimately achieve the goal of cost reduction.

(2) Through the cooperation of logistics alliance members, redundant institutions can be streamlined. The efficiency of streamlined institutions can be improved, thus achieving the goal of efficiency enhancement.

(3) The logistics alliance could form a solid organizational structure after a long-term cooperation among its members. The members of the alliance rely on each other and cooperate for win-win results. The established mechanisms of cooperation and trust help to mitigate risks of dishonesty and irresponsible behavior, thus enhancing the stability of the alliance.

(4) The logistics alliance could enhance the market competitiveness. After the logistics alliance stabilizes its operations, cuts costs and boosts efficiency, the increased market competitiveness would enable it to be in a better position to tap into logistics resources at lower prices, secure more market resources at lower rates, and achieve superior expansion results for the alliance.

From the perspective of external environment, the advantages of logistics alliance are as follows:

(1) Building a logistics alliance is good to achieve economies of scale, acquire external resources at a lower cost, and improve efficiency while reducing expenses. The effective implementation of the Cross-border E-commerce logistics alliance model can significantly reduce operational costs. However, this can't be achieved without the support and services provided by the necessary infrastruc-

ture. Thanks to the support and assistance provided by government agencies. China's Cross-border E-commerce logistics infrastructure has undergone significant improvement in recent years. As a result, the operating costs for the Cross-border E-commerce logistics alliance model have been continuously decreasing.

(2) The formation of a logistics alliance enables member companies to work together, expand their market share and increase market capacity. Through the integration of resources and coordinated cooperation within the logistics alliance, companies can quickly enter new markets, engage in Cross-border business, and gain more orders and revenue. As the market expands, companies can better share market risks and enhance their competitiveness.

(3) The Cross-border logistics alliance allows for better utilization of resources in both domestic and foreign markets. It broadens the scope of resource allocation, targets resources in the global market, and enables worldwide resource allocation.

4. 2. 2. 3　Strategy for Optimization of Cross-border Logistics Alliance

At present, China's Cross-border logistics alliance is still in the process of transitioning from the intermediate to the advanced stage. It faces challenges in forming a stable synergistic management system among its members, as there are significant conflicts of interest and difficulty in coordinating interests of various parties. The main reason of the constant friction is the absence of a central coordination mechanism to balance the interests of the members. Given this, even if the alliance relationship is maintained, true cooperation can not be achieved. Additionally, the membership of the alliance is randomly assembled, the organizational structure is loose, and there is a lack of necessary information sharing and communication mechanisms, making it difficult for the alliance to achieve stable and long-term development. Therefore, China's optimization plan for Cross-border logistics alliance will begin with optimizing the top-level design of the logistics alliance.

In terms of optimizing the top-level strategy of the logistics alliance, Jiang Yunfang (2022) proposed the creation of a governing body like the "Cross-border Logistics Management Bureau". This bureau could manage and support companies within the Cross-border E-commerce logistics alliance through a comprehensive support network of both the central and local governments.

After the central government establishes the governing body, local governments can take the lead in engaging with local businesses, and establish specialized and integrated local industrial parks through enterprise investment and government support. This will drive the development of local Cross-border logistics centers and create regional specialized industrial clusters. For instance, China established Ximeng Airport Logistics Park at the end of 2022, featuring a property rights trading platform, motor vehicle inspection service platform, and logistics information platform. Under government coordination, it planned and implemented an express logistics center and a multi-modal transportation center. The park has successfully integrated Cross-border E-commerce cold-chain transportation, logistics distribution and commercial circulation, resulting in a 30% reduction in transportation costs for the Cross-border E-commerce logistics alliance. Another example is the Erdos Airport Logistics Park, established in 2012. It is an autonomous region-level key industrial park integrating various functions, such as airport and land harbour, comprehensive bonded zones, processing and manufacturing center, modern logistics and E-commerce center. The successful integration of the modern logistics service industry is exemplified by its notable sales revenue of 2. 21 billion *yuan* attained in the year 2021.

The "central + local government" support model goes well in solving the domestic issues of Cross-border E-commerce. However, the Cross-border logistics alliance also involves crossing border issues. To ensure smooth international trade, governments should strengthen consultations with foreign governments and establish a normalized mechanism of economic cooperation. This mechanism should primarily focus on resolving common trade disputes, such as tariffs and trade barriers. Additionally, measures should be taken to prevent negative impacts on the Cross-border E-commerce logistics alliance from sudden changes in the trade environment. Practical actions should be taken to eliminate or shorten institutional distance.

Other than government's policy support, the logistics alliance also needs to improve its management capabilities internally. Firstly, the logistics alliance should create an innovative Cross-border logistics alliance comprehensive service platform. The core of the Cross-border E-commerce logistics ecosystem is a comprehensive service platform with automated and information-based operational capabilities. Cross-border E-commerce logistics alliance should provide specialized Cross-border services through the platform and achieve cost reduction and efficiency gains. It should continuously innovate the operational modes within the Cross-border logistics alliance, and build an innovative comprehensive service platform for efficient operation under the "Internet Cross-border logistics + " model.

For example, as early as the beginning of 2019, JD Cloud Warehouse, a subsidiary of JD Logistics, has begun to plan the establishment of a cloud logistics platform, providing "logistics flow + goods flow" solutions for overseas partners, reducing storage cost, and improving the transportation level, cargo handling and capacity of Cross-border E-commerce logistics. Through the platform-based logistics alliance model, Cross-border logistics has realized the goal of cost reduction and efficiency enhancement. On January 3rd, 2019, Parcelway Cross-border Supply Chain Comprehensive Service Platform signed contracts with multiple logistics companies, including Shenzhen SpeedEx, CJ GLS, Yunsu Supply Chain Management, YueFeng Logistics, and Equick. This partnership marks a new phase of development for the Cross-border E-commerce logistics alliance. By collaborating with those companies, Parcelway Cross-border Supply Chain Comprehensive Service Platform is able to meet consumers' logistics needs, improve logistics delivery efficiency, and reduce logistics costs in a better way.

The COVID-19 pandemic brought about a significant development in Cross-border E-commerce. However, by the end of 2022, with the global pandemic gradually coming to an end, the industry saw adjustments and a decline in performance. In April 2021, Amazon launched a large-scale store account closure. While in 2022, PayPal implemented an "Account Freeze" policy for independent DTC e-retailers. The US Patent and Trademark Office also imposed sanctions on tens of thousands of Chinese trademarks. Shipping prices from China to the US West Coast plummeted, and carriers still struggled to fill their containers. At the same time, leading DTC companies in the US saw their stock prices collectively plummet, while other top-tier firms like Amazon, Alibaba, and ByteDance undergoing mass layoffs, business optimization, and strategic contraction. Additionally, a few Canadian E-commerce platforms and service providers Shopify experienced layoffs and a drop in stock prices. International business expansion of E-commerce platforms, such as JD. com and Southeast Asian E-commerce platform Shopee were hindered. Cross-border logistics and supply chain faces severe challenges. The year 2022 was a year of uncertainty for Cross-border E-commerce, and the international logistics and supply chain experienced significant volatility, resulting in the bankruptcy of logistics and supply chain companies. Looking ahead, the post-pandemic development of the international supply chain is expected to recover its prosperity state in 2019. This means that the supply chain will have to rely more on its intrinsic force to improve its structure, weather the global economic downturn, and find new growth opportunities over the coming years.

Secondly, promote the application of core technologies within the logistics alliance and build a digital Cross-border alliance system.

The core technology of intelligent logistics should be applied within the logistics alliance, with the aim of reducing transportation security risks through the digital tracking system. This system visualizes the operation processes of the Cross-border E-commerce logistics alliance model. Cross-border E-commerce logistics alliance in China should proactively seek for domestic and foreign smart technologies to enhance the efficiency of the model. In recent years, Cross-border E-commerce logistics enterprises have adopted many new technologies, which have significantly improved the digitalization of the Cross-border E-commerce logistics alliance model, reduced operating costs and enhanced logistics efficiency. For instance, Alibaba's acquisition of Lazada, the largest E-commerce platform in Southeast Asia, enabled the construction of its own "Lazada wallet + cash on delivery" payment system, and thus connected Cross-border online shopping and payment.

The Cross-border logistics alliance is utilizing core technology to develop a digital Cross-border alliance system. By leveraging big data, the alliance can better cater to the needs of small-and medium-sized Cross-border E-commerce enterprises by providing personalized services. As more small- medium- and mini-sized enterprises engage in Cross-border E-commerce logistics business, the demand for comprehensive Cross-border logistics services is rapidly increasing. Cross-border logistics comprehensive service providers would capitalize on their advantages in information technology and resource integration to standardize and digitalize Cross-border logistics processes, and offer integrated professional services, such as clearance, tax, exchange settlement, logistics, credit assurance and financing for small-and medium-sized enterprises (Qu Weixi and Wang Huimin, 2021). This improves their Cross-border logistics efficiency while simultaneously solving the financing and development difficulties for these logistics enterprises.

Finally, the logistics alliance should standardize the logistics alliance cooperation agreement and establish a coordinated management mechanism.

Due to the complexity of internal organization in Cross-border logistics alliances, the highest level of risk of its operation is the coordination and management risk, also known as the collaboration risk. This risk lowers efficiency, and it may even jeopardize the existence of the alliance. To truly mitigate coordination and management risk, alliance enterprises need to establish a coordinated management mechanism to standardize the behavior of all parties involved. This mechanism requires all parties involved to sign a cooperation agreement by increasing the cohesion of cooperation and outlining the responsibilities and obligations of logistics alliance entities. This includes conflict settlement solutions, information sharing methods, and other aspects that limit corporate behavior for short-term profits, while enhancing the comprehensive management efficiency of the organization. Organizing an alliance management committee can improve the management of Cross-border logistics alliances (Tian Qing and Li Guie, 2021). Members of the alliance should vote the committee to manage and supervise the alliance. The committee should also develop specific coordination and management mechanisms based on the actual division of labor among enterprises on the digital logistics platform to regulate the behavior of all parties. Secondly, by applying new technologies, such as blockchain, trust issues can be effectively resolved, and therefore reducing costs and improving efficiency. Only under the principle of cooperative benefits outweighing the costs, can the Cross-border E-commerce logistics alliance benefit its members. Alliance members complement each other's strengths and weaknesses, it is possible to achieve a sustainable development of the Cross-border E-commerce logistics alliance model. A sustainably developed alliance can provide long-term strategic planning, and thus ensuring the long-term and efficient operation of the model. However, it will be a long-term process of continuous refinement and optimization.

Chapter 5   Development Status and Optimization of Overseas Warehouse—A Multi-case Study

This chapter focuses on the significance and primary issues of overseas warehouses, and concentrates on the optimization strategies for them. Additionally, the cases of Western Post, Zongteng Group and Beijing Kaibo Jincheng Trade Co. , Ltd. are also examined.

5. 1   Introduction to Overseas Warehouse

Overseas warehouses have emerged with the development of Cross-border E-commerce. It refers to Cross-border E-commerce companies leasing or constructing warehouses in foreign countries, and sending the goods that need to be sold overseas in advance. Once a consumer places an order, the goods can be shipped directly from the overseas warehouse, effectively turning a long-distance Cross-border logistics into "last mile" delivery. The overseas warehouse model could effectively resolve the problems associated with Cross-border E-commerce direct mail mode. With the support of the first-leg transportation provided by overseas warehouses, the long-distance and complex Cross-border logistics could be simplified into last mile delivery in the destination country. As a result, user experience is significantly enhanced.

In terms of service provider, overseas warehouses can be divided into three types: the first type is the self-operated overseas warehouse built by large Cross-border E-commerce platforms, such as Tmall and JD; the second type is the third-party overseas warehouse leased by Cross-border sellers, which is constructed by logistics companies, such as SF Express and China Post; and the third type is the public overseas warehouse led by the government. Third-party overseas warehouses are the dominant players in the market. They are typically established and run by third-party logistics companies, providing a wide range of logistics services such as customs clearance, warehousing quality inspection, order acceptance, order sorting, multi-channel shipping, and subsequent transportation for many export-oriented Cross-border E-commerce enterprises.

5.2   Strategic Significance of Overseas Warehouse

In the *Report on the Work of the Government* (2022), it was proposed to accelerate the development of new forms and models of foreign trade, promote the development of Cross-border E-commerce, and support the construction of overseas warehouses. Cross-border E-commerce overseas warehouses, with their characteristics of localization, delayering and prompt delivery, have greatly facilitated domestic export enterprises to directly face overseas consumers, accelerating the transformation of foreign trade from simple processing and manufacturing exports to providing global customized supply chain services. The overseas warehouses are highly attractive to foreign trade enterprises. Overseas warehouses play a critical role in connecting the first-leg transportation of Cross-border logistics with the last mile distribution. Thanks to their powerful functions, they promote the functional improvement of last mile delivery and the integration of first-leg transportation. This, in turn, supports the healthy development of E-commerce platforms, encourages the transformation of international freight forwarders, and drives the industrial upgrading of traditional international trade. In short, overseas warehouses are not only essential overseas nodes for Cross-border E-commerce, but also crucial facilities that promote the overall coordinated development of the entire Cross-border logistics ecosystem. Being a recent development in Cross-border logistics, overseas warehouses can address numerous lingering challenges in this field. Furthermore, the emergence of overseas warehouses has catalyzed a shift in the Cross-border logistics thinking pattern from logistics-centric to supply chain-centric, making the overall integration of the Cross-border supply chain possible.

5.2.1 Promote Last Mile Functional Improvement and First-leg Qualitative Integration

Lu Xu (2016) highlighted the crucial role of third-party overseas warehouse construction in integrating Cross-border supply chains. Although overseas warehouses are situated in the middle of the Cross-border supply chain as a storage facility, they play a crucial role in facilitating the transformation of the first-leg transportation and enhancing the value-added functions of the last mile delivery. As a significant node in the middle tier of Cross-border logistics, the overseas warehouse has the potential of not only focusing on developing its own high-end value-added services, but also coordinating relationships among all parties involved. Furthermore, the overseas warehouse can also help streamline the last mile delivery, handle returns and exchanges, facilitate local sales of overstocked goods, expand the functions of the overseas warehouse beyond storage to encompass sales, and offer a comprehensive solution for both last mile delivery and reverse logistics. These all lead to a significant enhancement in the quality of last mile services provided by the overseas warehouse.

Moreover, overseas warehouses significantly impact first-leg transportation by enabling exporters to accurately forecast market demand, efficiently plan product selection, goods quantity, and destination for first-leg transport, timely anticipate replenishment quantity, and thus achieve a transformative integration of firstleg logistics.

5. 2. 2   Promote the Growth of Cross-border E-commerce Platforms

As a trade intermediary, the Cross-border E-commerce platform connects manufacturers and overseas consumers. By incorporating overseas warehouses, the Cross-border E-commerce platform is able to provide a better customer experience, offer more competitive prices, and generate relatively higher profits. Additionally, the centralized management of exported goods in the overseas warehouse, along with its strict supervision, helps to mitigate a significant portion of Cross-border E-commerce trade disputes and maintain the reputation of the E-commerce platform, thus driving its growth.

5. 2. 3   Promote the Transformation of International Freight Forwarders

As of January 2022, the statistics on shipping in China revealed that there were over 60,000 enterprises engaging in the freight forwarding business, and they were seriously homogenized. The emergence of overseas warehouses provides a good opportunity for the transformation of international freight forwarders. By integrating sea freight, air freight, postal and international commercial express, traditional international freight forwarders can enhance their Cross-border transportation efficiency. Furthermore, forwarders can also extend to Cross-border warehousing, build overseas warehouses, and develop value-added services. It's safe to say that overseas warehouses represent the most promising path for the transformation of international freight forwarders.

5.3　The Function and Profile of Chinese Overseas Warehouse

The seller's logic behind using overseas warehouses is to predict future sales volume based on market demand, population, development level of economy, and other factors, and send a certain quantity of goods to the overseas warehouses ahead of time. This streamlines the last mile delivery process, reduces time cost associated with customs clearance and commodity inspection. The bulk and large scale transportation can effectively minimize risks and lower costs throughout the transportation process(Xie Jiahao,2022).

Besides delivering goods in destination country, the overseas warehouse also offers a fast handling of returns and exchanges. By utilizing overseas warehouses, Cross-border E-commerce sellers can provide buyers with better and more convenient after-sales services. Moreover, the overseas warehouse can also offer repackaging and other services for returned items, facilitating the resale of these products.

The overseas warehouse, once approved by customs to become a bonded warehouse, has a wider range of functions and applications. It simplifies the customs clearance process and related paperwork. Additionally, transit trade can also be carried out in the bonded warehouse. In this case, the overseas warehouse, as a third party, connects both the seller's and buyer's countries. The bonded overseas warehouse can further provide additional value-added services, such as basic processing, more than just repackaging of returned goods. These effectively enhance the warehousing capabilities and improve resource utilization efficiency.

As of the end of 2021, China has constructed over 2,000 overseas warehouses with a total area of over 16 million square meters. [1] These warehouses continue to improve their functions and promote the development of Cross-border E-commerce and foreign trade in China. Chinese government has always been supporting the development of overseas warehouses, and various departments and administrative agencies have actively been cooperating in this endeavor. The Ministry of Commerce, together with other relevant departments, has proposed eight guidelines and circulars to support the development of overseas warehouses, setting up special funds like the Foreign Trade Development Special Funds, as well as the Service Trade Innovation and Development Guidance Fund to support the construction of overseas warehouses and optimize the record-filing process for better supervision.

Local customs authorities have also issued relevant supportive policies. As Tianjin Customs has taken the initiative to speed up the reform for new business formats and modes, opening a fast channel for overseas warehouse businesses, simplifying record-filing procedures. [2]Through hotline, online platforms, and other "time-saving" and "contactless" communication channels, Tianjin Customs provides "one-to-one" guidance for enterprises interested in opening overseas warehouse. These efforts have enabled local enterprises to upgrade and improve their Cross-border E-commerce exports to secure orders and stabilize expectations. [3]Qianjiang Customs in Zhejiang Province has also actively supported overseas warehouse export businesses by promoting the "Ten Regions, Hundreds of Teams Helping Thousands of Enterprises" initiative, which aims to assist targeted enterprises in their export business. Additionally, the Ministry of Commerce has been promoting the nationwide networking of information, enabling "local record-filing, nationwide acceptance," and supporting overseas warehouses in optimizing their market layout. This enables them to function more intelligently as multifunc-

---

[1]   https://baijiahao. baidu. com/s? id = 1730704858541044415&wfr = spider&for = pc, 23 - 1 - 2023.

[2]   http://www. gov. cn/xinwen/2022zccfh/26/index. htm,23 - 1 - 2023.

[3]   http://news. enorth. com. cn/system/2022/11/20/053352730. shtml,23 - 1 - 2023.

tional service platforms. Furthermore, the Ministry has been continuously introducing supportive measures for overseas warehouses to aid their development.

Zhang Zengfu (2022) used the TOPSIS method to measure and analyze the development status and comprehensive service capacity of 35 influential Cross-border E-commerce enterprises in China. His research figures show that 20 of the 35 enterprises have a measurement value higher than the average, and the comprehensive service capacity of the top Cross-border E-commerce overseas warehouse enterprises is 3. 747 (0. 993/0. 265) times that of the bottom ones. These figures show that there are significant disparities in China's Cross-border E-commerce overseas warehouse service capacity, and the overall development level is highly uneven.

Although the concept of overseas warehouses seems as a new focus, the industry has actually been developing for several years and has already experienced intense competition. Without the COVID-19 pandemic in 2020, many overseas warehouse companies would be difficult to sustain. During the pandemic, the limitations in international supply chain management and transportation capacity were highlighted. Overseas warehouses and bonded warehouses, as a supplement to the stocking system, played a crucial role in mitigating the impact of the pandemic on Cross-border E-commerce sellers' overseas inventory. These facilities have advantages in localized operations, logistics distribution efficiency, and convenient return and exchange to maintain their sustained prosperity during the pandemic. Local governments have implemented supportive policies to encourage the construction of overseas warehouses. In April 2020, the Ningbo government offered loans at a 4% annual interest rate, with a minimum term of two years and a 50% interest discount for enterprises building their own overseas warehouses. [1] In January 2023, the Tianjin government implemented 33 policies to stabilize the economy and encourage enterprises to jointly build and share overseas warehou-

---

[1]   http://www. ningbo. gov. cn/art/2020/4/20/art_1229187964_53685590. html, 25 – 1 – 2023.

ses. Overseas warehouses invested by enterprises or public warehouses leased by enterprises, with a storage area of over 2,000 square meters in a single country or region, may receive up to 1 million *yuan* in financial support. [1]

But the pandemic was only a short-term stimulus. The fleeting prosperity ended in the first half of 2021. In the second half of 2021, overseas warehouses began to lower prices and engage in internal competition, and they faced many new challenges. Firstly, when international freight forwarders transformed their business to overseas warehouses, their thinking pattern did not transform accordingly. They still followed the traditional concept of charging fees based on the value of goods, seeking more profits by taking more physical cargoes. This resulted in numerous Cross-border E-commerce companies mindlessly rushed into the overseas warehouse business, which led to a flood of goods unsuited for local markets being shipped to overseas warehouses. Goods were stuck in storage and, in some cases, even abandoned or destroyed because of an inability to cover storage fees. This situation had a significant impact on the overseas warehouse experience of exporting companies (Lu Xu, 2016). Overseas warehouses were originally introduced as a crucial Cross-border E-commerce logistics solution to balance the logistics costs and efficiency for such companies. However, that is not the case in reality, overseas warehouse companies are now under immense market pressure. To cut cost, some of these companies have resorted to lowering their service quality and focusing on the low-end market, which could result in customer loss and threaten the long-term growth of the company.

Additionally, the emergence of "virtual overseas warehouses" is also a response to market pressure. Virtual overseas warehouses is a technology-simulated concept. They achieve fast delivery and low logistics costs by partnering with domestic express companies. Although virtual overseas warehouses can attract customers in the short term, their after-sales services often have problems, such as

---

[1]　http://app. myzaker. com/news/article. php? pk =63e246b98e9f0930cc51f05e,23 -1 -2023.

non-existent physical overseas storage services and low quality after-sales services. Furthermore, virtual overseas warehouses carry the "sin" of deceiving consumers, once exposed, they will face serious legal risks.

Currently, a healthy Cross-border logistics ecosystem is not yet in place. As a result, overseas warehouses continue to face severe internal competition and friction. Furthermore, even well-established overseas warehouse enterprises still face a host of specific challenges in their operational processes.

5.4   Challenges Faced by Overseas Warehouse Enterprises

Overall, the products and services of China's Cross-border logistics enterprises are seriously homogenized and lack of core competitiveness. If overseas enterprises want to stand out, they must build their own competitive barriers and improve their core competitiveness. The construction of these warehouses requires substantial investment, yet the output does not match the investment. The main problems are discussed in the following aspects.

5.4.1   Low Localization Level

One major trend in overseas warehouse development is localization, but there are several challenges that need to be addressed. Firstly, studying the local policies, particularly the tax policy, is crucial. As business entities, overseas warehouses need to closely comply with local tax policies. However, tax policies vary significantly among different regions. The complexity of tax policies can lead to a wrong taxation which creates troubles for overseas warehouse enterprises. Secondly, local recruitment is difficult. Employing domestic employees in overseas warehouses involves complex visa and residency issues. So to localize operations, hiring local workers is more practical. In developed countries like the European countries and the United States, labor costs are higher than those in developing countries. For instance, blue-collar workers' hourly wages are around ＄20. High wages and tipping culture make it more difficult to hire local employees. Thirdly, localized marketing is not easy. Customers' needs vary in different countries. It is challenging to provide tailored products and accurate pricing strategies to them. However, the real challenge lies in precise cross-cultural marketing. Different countries have significant cultural and behavioral differences, which makes targeted marketing and platform traffic guiding difficult (Xie Guimei, 2022).

5. 4. 2   Low Customer Satisfaction

Currently, Cross-border E-commerce logistics costs account for 20% to 30% of the total costs. Cross-border logistics investment is high, but customer satisfaction is low. According to FocalPrice's customer satisfaction survey, customers' complaints about Cross-border E-commerce are mainly on logistics. [1] Even the overseas warehouses set up by the leading domestic Cross-border E-commerce platforms failed to achieve high customer satisfaction. Xiong Jun and Zhu Siyi (2021) studied the distribution of major logistics problems in overseas warehouses taking Kaibo Jincheng Ltd. as an example, and found that 51% of customer dissatisfaction was caused by product return and exchange. So untimely response to goods return and exchange is the major reason of low customer satisfaction. When buyers choose to return or exchange the goods, they have to wait for 2 weeks to have their requirements processed. The slow order processing system leads to low efficiency in logistics and therefore poor consumer experience. On the other hand,

---

[1]   https://business. sohu. com/a/584830766_121333014,2023 – 1 – 23; https://wenhui. whb. cn/third/baidu/201910/21/295936. html,2023 – 1 – 23.

companies have difficulty in accurately understanding customer needs. When dealing with customers from various countries and regions, it is crucial to take into account the differences in language, culture, customs and consumer behavior. Unfortunately, employees of overseas warehouse companies often lack the necessary cross-cultural awareness and abilities. As a result, accurately understanding the needs of local customers becomes challenging, leading to a mismatch in product research and development, design, marketing, and distribution. Ultimately, this results in an unsatisfactory online shopping experience for consumers.

5. 4. 3   Low Logistics Ecological Coordination

In the Cross-border logistics and supply chain ecosystem, overseas warehouse enterprises need to go beyond simply ensuring the smooth running of the supply chain, they must also provide integrated and collaborative services in payment, customs clearance, tax payment, finance, laws and regulations. These services have a direct impact on delivery speed, capital security, customs clearance efficiency and tax compliance. Despite these crucial roles, China's overseas warehouse enterprises still grapple with challenges when it comes to the ecosystem coordination. One of the difficulties faced by Cross-border logistics is the low efficiency of customs clearance. Overseas warehouse businesses are typically high in volume of order but low in unit price, which can lead to frequent yet complicated procedures including customs clearance, goods inspection and supervision, etc. This is particularly problematic for Cross-border E-commerce, which requires faster customs clearance. Such contradictions may increase uncertainty into the customs clearance process, exacerbating the issue further. During the customs clearance process in destination countries, overseas warehouses encounter various challenges, including differences in customs management regulations and complicated clearance procedures. The wide range of products in Cross-border E-commerce, coupled with the need for frequent clearance, can make inspections more difficult, leading to a lower efficiency. Currently, many E-commerce companies handle the declaration and clearance procedures on their own, without the assistance of professional clearance companies. This often results in increased uncertainty during the clearance process.

5. 4. 4   Low Logistics Integration

The overseas warehouse serves as a vital link connecting first-leg transportation and last mile delivery in the destination country, and the seamless integration and connection of different logistics stages are critical to the smooth operation and cost-effectiveness of the overseas warehouse. However, the current state of Cross-border logistics integration remains relatively low in three key areas. Firstly, the cost of first-leg transportation is high. First-leg transportation generally refers to the rail, air and sea transportation, or a combination of them, to transport goods in bulk to overseas warehouses in destination countries. First-leg transportation includes domestic transportation, ocean transportation and part of transportation in overseas country, involving Cross-border transportation, customs clearance and inspection procedures. Different customs clearance procedures in various countries are complex. As a result, E-commerce companies that attempt to manage first-leg transportation on their own are bound to bear high costs and risks. Secondly, the operating cost of overseas warehouses is high. The upfront investment for self-built overseas warehouses is huge, and the operating cost is high, which is only suitable for top-tier E-commerce companies. For most other small E-commerce companies, choosing to lease overseas warehouses is a better option. The operating cost of overseas warehouses is relatively high, mainly concentrated in labor, energy consumption and rental cost. However, extensive duplication in warehouse construction leads to inefficient resource utilization and significant waste. Lastly, the value-added services level offered by most overseas warehouses is low. The current services are just goods sorting, packaging and other basic services, with a low level of added value. Most importantly, these services do not cover the services that sellers are most concerned about, such as returns, exchanges and repairs. So sellers have to send their products back to the import country for replacement or repair, which ultimately leads to an increase in sellers' costs.

5. 4. 5　Low Digitalization Level

The Cross-border E-commerce business continues to grow, but the digitalization level of overseas warehouses has not been improved accordingly, which seriously limits the development of Cross-border E-commerce business. During the early stages of overseas warehouse development, the volume of business was relatively small, and goods were usually stored in a warehouse or even just in a garage. When there is an order, delivery could be arranged. The early operating process was simple. However, this workshop-style operation is only suitable for small-scale inventory and order volumes. Once the order volume surges, problems such as incorrect shipments, inaccurate inventory, expensive terminal delivery, inability to conduct reverse logistics, poor after-sales service, uncertain delivery vehicles, and inability to intelligently allocate shipments according to warehouse addresses will inevitably arise, leading to a delivery disorder of overseas warehouses. To ensure efficient operations in the current global E-commerce landscape, overseas warehouses must maintain a high level of digitalization to promptly respond to various logistics links (Wang Lihe *et al.* ,2022). A popular system used by such companies, including Kaibo Jincheng Ltd., is ERP (Enterprise Resource Planning), which unfortunately relies heavily on manual review and lacks big data integration, causing delays in logistics information tracking and shipment errors. To avoid such issues, it is necessary to standardize and digitize storage and distribution management with systems like WMS, scanning guns, in-and-out stock management and picking path setting. Zhang Zengfu (2021) designed a measurement index system for the service capability of overseas warehouses, with the highest weights given to transaction volume and automation level, indicating that the scale and information service capability of overseas warehouses determine their overall service capability.

To summarize, the construction of overseas warehouses requires a significant amount of capital investment within a short time frame. Since the warehouses are scattered in different locations, achieving economies of scale to reduce costs is challenging. It requires substantial financial support. Additionally, the construction process is lengthy, and the return on investment is slow, making it difficult for small- and medium-sized businesses to bear (Ge Yan, 2016). If the localization level of the overseas warehouses is insufficient, issues caused by institutional policies and cultural differences may emerge, leading to the failure of warehouse integration into local operations. These may cause the management problems and localization problems, contributing to the low customer satisfaction to overseas warehouse services. Even for the overseas warehouse set up by top-tier companies, operational issues cannot be solved in a short period. China has many small- and medium-sized enterprises participating in Cross-border E-commerce operations. Considering these national conditions, it is more suitable for the government to lead the construction of public overseas warehouses to promote sustainable development.

5.5   Optimization of Overseas Warehouse Operation Model

Building and operating overseas warehouses require a huge investment of capital and a deep understanding of the target market's culture, policies, regulations and industry standards. It also demands the ability to manage global logistics. The development of overseas warehouses faces both macro and micro risks and challenges. As Cross-border E-commerce continues to grow and penetrate, the potential of China's Cross-border market remains massive, and the future outlook is still positive. Although intense competitions (external or internal) exist temporarily, the opportunities in the Cross-border logistics industry outweigh the challenges. As of December 2021, China had over 2,000 overseas warehouses with a total area of more than 16 million square meters, accumulating a certain amount of experience and a solid foundation. Nearly 90% of these warehouses are located in North America, Europe and Asia. These figures prove that the trend of developing overseas warehouses will remain unchanged, but their operating model needs further optimization.

From a macro perspective, it's challenging for Cross-border logistics third-party companies to independently build an overseas warehouse strategy without government support. To address this issue, the State Council released the *14th Five-Year Plan for the Development of Modern Logistics* in December 2022, calling for an accelerated deployment of enterprise self-built overseas warehouses and a steady improvement of overseas logistics network services. As noted by Lu Xu (2016), besides offering financing support, the government must guide and encourage warehouse-related service industries, such as insurance, legal, financial, consulting, and information, to *go out* and expand globally. The government and companies should work together to build Cross-border logistics and supply chain dominated by third-party logistics companies. Cross-border logistics companies can make full use of the government's support policies for the development of overseas warehouses, bravely explore new locations, avoid clustering in warehouse locations, and choose regions with good political environments and promising trade prospects for warehouse construction, such as countries along the " two sides (coastside and borderside) and ten corridors (international logistics channels) " and countries in the Regional Comprehensive Economic Partnership (RCEP) region. In China's key regions for Cross-border trade, Yang Jie (2022) proposed that large logistics companies should work together to establish overseas warehouses through various means, including setting up funds, to provide services for small-and medium-sized enterprises that struggle to build their own overseas warehouses. As the overseas warehouse business expands, new things like "virtual overseas warehouses" have emerged. To ensure proper alignment with Cross-border logistics regulations, it is crucial to operate within the boundaries of the rules, including those related to "virtual overseas warehouses". Therefore, as the overseas warehouse industry continues to evolve, standardized management of innovation must be strengthened. This includes further regulating overseas warehouse service standards and operating norms from the top-level design for Cross-border E-commerce to enhance the level of compliance and provide professional guidance for building and operating overseas warehouses.

The above is the macro-level construction of the policy environment for Cross-border E-commerce, which involves the development of policies, strengthened supervision, standardization, international collaboration, as well as the protection of Intellectual Property Rights, risk management, and the cultivation of Cross-border E-commerce talents. Such institutional environment can foster the healthy growth of Cross-border E-commerce, enhance its marketing strength, reduce transaction risks and costs, and elevate its global competitiveness.

From a micro perspective, overseas warehouse enterprises must greatly enhance their collaboration within the logistics ecosystem by effectively working together with entities, such as logistics companies, warehousing companies, customs, inspection, tax, payment platforms and others. They must also improve and engage more deeply in the local operation, and utilize information technology to do precise local marketing while raising cross-cultural business awareness. They also need to improve their logistics integration level by integrating and consolidating services, such as quality management, marketing promotion, channel construction, logistics transportation, warehousing distribution, customs declaration and inspection, payment settlement, and after-sales service. Although the overseas warehouse is the final stop in the entire Cross-border E-commerce ecosystem, it is the core module of the ecosystem. It is crucial to build a smart, stable and efficient full-link Cross-border logistics ecosystem. The following part discusses the optimization of the overseas warehouse business model from five aspects: logistics ecological synergy capability, localization operation capability, logistics integration capability, intelligent operation capability, and customer service enhancement capability, based on the construction of the logistics ecosystem.

5.5.1 Logistics Ecological Synergy Capability

Efficient operation of the entire Cross-border logistics ecosystem can only be realized when all its links cooperate with each other seamlessly. To achieve the convenient and efficient operation of each chain in the ecosystem, it is essential to jointly improve the coordination of payment and settlement, customs clearance and taxation, finance. It connects all links such as capital security, customs clearance, logistics speed, and tax payment compliance, and therefore impacts the overall functioning of the ecosystem. A plenty of studies focus on the synergy of logistics ecosystem, such as the synergistic movements of each chain (Du Zhiping, 2018, 2020; Zhang Xiaheng, 2016; Zhang Xiaheng, Zhang Ronggang, 2018). It also includes more detailed studies, mainly focusing on customs clearance efficiency and compliance operations (Xiong Jun, 2021; Wang Lihe *et al.* , 2022). To enhance customs clearance efficiency, it's essential to take proactive measures such as improving communication with international agencies and government departments, and encouraging countries to align with international customs supervision standards. Cross-border E-commerce companies should also explore ways to streamline their customs clearance processes for greater convenience. For instance, they could consider setting up company-owned customs clearance companies to manage their customs operations more efficiently and professionally. There are several successful cases. As early as 2016, as a comprehensive service provider of the entire logistics chain from China to Europe and the United States, Western Post Logistics set up four independent customs clearance subsidiaries in the United States, the United Kingdom, Germany and Belgium. Zongteng Group also focuses on promoting "end-to-end overseas fulfillment supply chain services" in 2022, [1] including overseas international truck lines, and providing specialized services such as overseas customs clearance and overseas distribution. [2]

Another aspect of logistics ecosystem synergy is compliance with tax regulations. It requires understanding the tax policies of the destination country and establishing communication and cooperation with local tax authorities to create a legal ecosystem for overseas warehouses. In the operation of overseas warehouses, Cross-border E-commerce enterprises should identify their role as the principal entity and actively learn about the tax policies in the destination country to pay taxes in compliance with the law. Xiong Jun and Zhu Siyi (2021) emphasized that Cross-border E-commerce enterprises can enhance tax payment efficiency by promoting the computerization of tax supervision methods and adapting to new E-commerce business formats. In international cooperation, it is essential to promote tax cooperation among governments, implement electronic taxation procedures, and produce mutually accepted receipts to avoid double taxation.

5. 5. 2   Localization Operation Capability

According to Xiao Liang *et al.* (2019), a strong localized operation capability is key to a Cross-border E-commerce company's overall success. This capability is measured through three important dimensions: local logistics service, local distribution service and local conflict coordination. Each of these factors highlights a

---

① Fujian Zongteng Internet Co. Ltd (Zongteng) was established in 2009. It is a global Cross-border ecommerce infrastructure service provider, focusing on cross border warehousing and international logistics. It provides services of overseas warehousing, commercial special line and customerized service. It has YunExpress, Goodcang, Worldtech one-stop service etc.

② https://baijiahao. baidu. com/s? id = 1739688458425636340&wfr = spider&for = pc, 2023 – 1 – 25.

company's ability to adapt to the unique needs of the target market. In the first dimension, local logistics service, a company must be able to respond quickly to the logistical needs of the destination country, including efficient warehousing, distribution and return services. The second dimension, local distribution service, emphasizes that enterprises should effectively utilize and integrate distribution resources in the destination country to offer efficient marketing, including brand promotion, product sales, channel services, product display and trial service. The third and final dimension, local conflict coordination, demands a company to use relationship resources within the destination country to settle any conflicts and disputes that may arise, ensuring that the company operates smoothly within the market. Overall, to achieve long-term success in Cross-border E-commerce, a company must continuously strive to improve its localization capabilities across all three dimensions.

The localized operation capability is a complex and multi-faceted capability, encompassing the ability to build local warehouses as well as the capability to operate effectively after a warehouse is built. Firstly, for Cross-border E-commerce companies, establishing a localized operation and management team and hiring more local workforce is critical to success. Each country has different cultures and policies, and locals are more familiar with their own country's culture but not with that of the destination country. It is difficult for foreign workers to adapt their mindset to understand local culture in a short time. Thus, forming a localized team is crucial for truly achieving localized operations. Secondly, Cross-border E-commerce companies should also provide localized services package in local language, such as localized payment methods and localized last mile delivery, by selecting the right third-party payment platform and storing sufficient quantity of goods in local warehouses. This requires that Cross-border E-commerce enterprises have a deep insight into local customs, law and regulation system, and consumption preference and do a precision marketing. As to localized payment, they must be cautious in selecting a third-party payment platform and offering local payment interface to realize a localized payment. In localized delivery, they should have appropriate quantity of goods in local warehouse and deliver them locally to reduce logistics steps and improve efficiency and revenue. Western Post is a good example of successful localized operation, with over 25 self-operated warehouses located in countries such as the United States, Germany and the United Kingdom. They have formed local business clusters in places like Los Angeles, New Jersey, Houston, Chicago and Atlanta. [1]

5.5.3　Logistics Integration Capability

The function of an overseas warehouse is not limited to storage. It is closely connected with the first-leg sea and air shipping, and last mile B2B bulk distribution and B2C parcel delivery. The integration of those is an inevitable trend for overseas warehouses to reduce costs and improve efficiency. Companies can take advantage of sea shipping to achieve low-cost transportation in the first-leg transportation, and then store their goods in overseas warehouses for centralized management. These warehouses also offer value-added services, such as simple packaging and repackaging. When customers place an order, quick delivery can be made through localized logistics systems. This not only improves delivery speed but also enhances customer experience and satisfaction. Therefore, localized delivery is a significant advantage of overseas warehouses. Integrating various functions will further enhance these advantages and make them even more beneficial for businesses.

The integrated operation of overseas warehouses involves continuously improving the ability to integrate logistics resources and enhancing the synergy of Cross-border logistics. This is achieved by analyzing the unique product characteristics,

---

[1]　https://baijiahao.baidu.com/s? id = 1734968764357734093&wfr = spider&for = pc, 25 - 1 - 2023.

business areas, and transportation requirements. From there, partnerships with specialized third-party logistics providers such as ocean, rail and road transport, as well as local logistics companies, are sought to address the finer details of first-and last-leg transportation. To ensure successful first-leg transportation, different transportation modes are flexibly combined according to the location of the destination country and the characteristics of the transported goods. Meanwhile, cooperation with local logistics companies ensures a timely and efficient delivery for the last mile fulfillment. Western Post is a successful example of exploring the construction of localized logistics capabilities and continuously improving its customized services. Western Post has its own truck team to complete local logistics tasks, which provides more convenient scheduling when picking up goods from the port. This advantage was particularly evident during the COVID-19 pandemic period when there was a severe shortage of truck drivers. Furthermore, Western Post's self-operated truck team can reduce distribution costs during last mile delivery. There are many similar companies that operate their own transportation networks, and some international warehouse leaders have started investing in improving their sea and air transportation capabilities. For example, Zongteng Group had its first Boeing wide-body cargo aircraft B777F flight to Riyadh Airport in Saudi Arabia. [1] This operation allowed Zongteng to secure a more self-sustaining capacity, thereby improving the stability of its supply chain services.

For specific segmented categories and customer groups, the government encourages overseas warehouse companies to build specialized overseas warehouses, such as warehouses for large items, SKD (Semi-Knocked-Down) warehouses, customized warehouses, and return and transit warehouses. For example, Western Post has been focusing on the warehousing service for large items for many years, specializing in "industry solutions for large items in Cross-border logistics" and mainly serving VIP brand customers. This competitive strategy has allowed Western

---

[1] https://www. dsb. cn/news-flash/102896. html,25 – 1 – 2023.

Post to easily navigate the industry's fluctuations. For Western Post, focusing on large items means giving up a higher proportion of small-item products, while focusing on mid-to-large-sized brand customers means giving up many small customers. However, it is this kind of focusing strategy that makes them set up a competitive barrier in just a few years, that is, "industrial solutions for large-sized products"[1]. In addition, Zongteng Group's "Zongteng-Gucang Overseas Warehouse" has also been developed for over a decade, focusing on developing large-sized categories such as furniture and auto parts to achieve warehousing specialization.

To enhance the capabilities of high-end value-added services, overseas warehouses have to take the advantages of local operations and develop value-added businesses accordingly. For instance, expanding inbound operations of overseas warehouses to customs clearance can greatly relieve customers' post-clearance worries. Similarly, adding basic value-added services like packaging management to warehouse management can help improve overall efficiency. Lu Xu (2016) suggested that, after goods are stored in the warehouse, overseas warehouses can partner with insurance companies and extend logistics services to include transportation and warehousing insurance coverage. Additionally, overseas warehouses can serve as tax payers, assisting Cross-border E-commerce firms with legal tax payment in the destination country. Overall, as a representative of exporters in the destination country, overseas warehouses need to coordinate among all parties.

5. 5. 4　Intelligent Operation Capability

Compared with traditional overseas warehouse, the most prominent merit of modern warehouse is the advancement in digitalization. Highly digitalized modern

---

[1]　https://baijiahao. baidu. com/s? id = 1731500414120735655&wfr = spider&for = pc, 25 − 1 − 2023.

overseas warehouse could realize intelligent operation and stocking under a visualized system. A digitalized and intelligent operational system helps a lot in indepth data mining, analysis of customer needs and preferences. Combined with information of the industry trend, product supplying capability, inventory allocation, the digital system could readjust product mix, marketing strategy and service plans. Wang Lihe *et al.* (2022) has outlined ten key components that make up this intelligent ecosystem: overall supply chain design, process management, marketing and product selection, demand forecasting, visual logistics, intelligent finance, procurement, warehousing, distribution and after-sales. These components are interconnected and form a comprehensive and intelligent ecosystem.

Western Post has applied intelligent logistics layout to enhance its operational capabilities. During peak promotional periods, many overseas warehouses were unable to book FedEx vehicles. As a result, order information could not be updated online, and thus influencing the seller's store performance. ① By intelligently calculating and distributing inventory to various warehouses, Western Post effectively fixed the vehicle shortage problem during the peak days. At the same time, the company has also laid out an intelligent visualization system in advance, enabling customers to clearly see the delivery data of each warehouse and assist in making distribution decisions. In the process of transporting goods from the factory to the overseas warehouse, Western Post has created 30 visual nodes to enable customers to track their shipment status in real-time. Western Post's success relies on their intelligent data system, which is supported by a dedicated team of IT professionals and an independently-developed system. The system includes a smart brain, operation platform, collaborative platform, transportation, warehousing, and transition functions. In other words, Western Post has a fully integrated system that covers the entire logistics chain, from first-leg transportation to port warehousing,

---

① https://baijiahao.baidu.com/s? id = 1731500414120735655&wfr = spider&for = pc, 2023 - 1 - 25.

warehousing entry, sorting, outbound delivery, and final distribution. This system is equipped with well-connected nodes and is capable of providing precise and transparent data throughout the entire process.

5.5.5   Customer Service Enhancement Capability

The implementation of an integrated and intelligent operation in overseas warehouses does not guarantee an automatic improvement in customer experience. As a local operator, overseas warehouses need to effectively improve their customer service capabilities. To avoid intense competition in a homogeneous industry, the overseas warehouses should adopt local marketing models, benchmark local competitors, increase customer stickiness and customer loyalty, and improve their competitiveness in destination markets. The top priority for managing overseas warehouses is to enhance customer satisfaction. The development philosophy of overseas warehouse enterprise is centered around customer needs. They should understand the culture and values of the destination country. In-depth research should be conducted to identify the unique needs, consumption psychology, and purchasing habits of local customers. Relevant data should be collected and analyzed to develop marketing and service strategies that align with customer preferences and improve their overall experience. Secondly, the service positioning must be precise. Overseas warehouse enterprises need to serve not only individual consumers but also small-and medium-sized enterprise customers. Therefore, warehousing and distribution capabilities should be clearly and precisely positioned. They should provide customized distribution services to meet customer's needs. Different industries have varying requirements for warehousing and logistics. For instance, some high-priced 3C electronic products require "unique code management" (each product has a unique code) to facilitate after-sales processing. With this service, sellers no longer need to deal with the malicious complaint about defective products and a request for a return. Currently, Western Post has established mature solutions in home furnishing, appliances, and 3C electronics industries. They offer complete and professional solutions to the reverse logistics of home furnishing and appliances, and to the "unique code management" of the high-end 3C electronic products. ①

---

① https://baijiahao. baidu. com/s? id = 1731500414120735655&wfr = spider&for = pc, 25 – 1 – 2023.

参考文献

［1］ ESTRIN S, BAGHDASARYAN D, MEYER K E. The impact of institutional and human resource distance on international entry strategies ［J］. Journal of Management Studies, 2009, 46 (7): 1171 – 1196.

［2］ GIUFFRIDA M, JIANG H, MANGIARACINA R. Investigating the relationships between uncertainty types and risk management strategies in cross-border ecommerce logistics ［J］. The International Journal of Logistics Management, 2021, 32 (4): 1406 – 1433.

［3］ PLACZEK E. New challenges for logistics providers in the e-business era ［J］. Electronic Scientific Journal of Logistics, 2010, 6 (2): 40 – 47.

［4］ 曹倩, 蒋晶. 跨境电商企业海外仓现状及风险对策研究 ［J］. 中国市场, 2022 (25): 180 – 182.

［5］ 曹武军, 闫梦娜, 薛朝改. 物流企业主导型跨境电商生态系统的构建: 多案例研究 ［J］. 科技管理研究, 2019 (16): 212 – 222.

［6］ 陈志娟. 数字经济对我国跨境电商规则的影响及完善对策 ［J］. 对外经贸实务, 2021 (09): 54 – 57.

［7］ 杜志平, 贡祥林. 国内外跨境物流联盟运作机制研究现状 ［J］. 中国流通经济, 2018, 32 (02): 37 – 49.

［8］ 杜志平, 区钰贤. 跨境电商供应链定价策略与协调决策机制研究: 基于组合契约模型的分析 ［J］. 价格理论与实践, 2020 (12): 119 – 122.

［9］ 杜志平. 跨境物流联盟运作机制与决策优化 ［M］. 北京: 首都经济贸易大学出版社, 2020.

［10］ 方思. 跨境电商背景下海外仓物流模式及选择策略研究 ［J］. 福建交通科技, 2020 (4): 173 – 176.

[11] 付帅帅，陈伟达，王丹丹．跨境电商物流供应链协同发展研究 [J]．东北大学学报（社会科学版），2021，23（01）：52–60．

[12] 高帆．跨境电商环境下跨境物流的潜在风险及防范：以万邦速达国际物流公司为例 [J]．对外经贸实务，2020（7）：77–80．

[13] 葛岩．跨境物流海外仓存在的问题及对策建议 [J]．山东财经大学学报，2016（3）：77–82．

[14] 郭文强，王彦博．基于行动思维规则的跨境电商海外仓模式选择研究 [J]．洛阳师范学院学报，2022，41（09）：43–59．

[15] 郭燕，王玉平．基于 PEST 分析的我国跨境电商竞争环境研究 [J]．情报探索，2020（01）：67–74．

[16] 韩玲冰，胡一波，王帅红．产业融合背景下的跨境电商与物流产业链融合发展分析 [J]．物流技术，2018（7）：20–22．

[17] 冀芳，张夏恒．跨境电子商务物流模式创新与发展趋势 [J]．中国流通经济，2015（6）：14–20．

[18] 江旭，姜飞飞．不确定性、联盟风险管理与合作绩效满意度 [J]．管理工程学报，2015，29（3）：180–190．

[19] 江运芳．新贸易形势下跨境电商物流联盟风险与防范 [J]．哈尔滨学院学报，2022，43（10）：61–65．

[20] 居永梅．跨境电商第三方物流选择的风险识别与评估 [J]．商业经济研究，2020（12）：82–84．

[21] 李航，黄昕怡．核心竞争力演化视角下我国跨境电商企业物流发展策略研究 [J]．商业经济研究，2021（21）：94–97．

[22] 李鹏博．揭秘跨境电商 [M]．北京：电子工业出版社，2015．

[23] 李实萍，崔毅．风险规避型航空联盟的收益共享机制研究 [J]．工业工程，2014，17（4）：47–62．

[24] 李旭东，曾艳英，王耀球．基于4PL的跨境电商物流联盟研究 [J]．商业经济研究，2017（7）：82–84．

[25] 李益帆，陈娟．数字经济背景下跨境电商物流的现状及发展策略 [J]．全国流通经济，2022（27）：14–16．

[26] 李元旭，罗佳．文化距离、制度距离与跨境电子商务中的感知风险 [J]．财经问题研究，2017（3）：106–114．

[27] 林子青. 跨境电商与跨境物流协同下的供应链生态模式及评价 [J]. 商业经济研究, 2020 (2): 152-155.

[28] 刘永胜, 王传阳. 基于风险识别的供应商选择 [J]. 统计与决策, 2012 (13): 51-53.

[29] 鲁旭. 基于跨境供应链整合的第三方物流海外仓建设 [J]. 中国流通经济, 2016 (3): 32-38.

[30] 马述忠, 郭继文. 数字经济时代的全球经济治理: 影响解构、特征刻画与取向选择 [J]. 改革, 2020 (1): 69-83.

[31] 米岩. 我国跨境电商发展模式优化机制研究: 基于供应链视角 [J]. 商业经济研究, 2022 (9): 136-140.

[32] 慕艳平. 我国跨境电商物流解决方案分析与选择 [J]. 物流技术, 2015, 34 (10): 83-84.

[33] 庞燕. 跨境电商环境下国际物流模式研究 [J]. 中国流通经济, 2015 (10): 15-20.

[34] 蒲新蓉. 数字经济时代跨境电商生态系统建设与发展策略 [J]. 质量与市场, 2022 (08): 160-162.

[35] 祁飞. 跨境电商国际物流模式的整合性问题探讨 [J]. 商业经济研究, 2020 (18): 113-115.

[36] 曲维玺, 王惠敏. 中国跨境电子商务发展态势及创新发展策略研究 [J]. 国际贸易, 2021 (03): 4-10.

[37] 权印. 跨境电商海外共享仓应用的必要性及实践途径 [J]. 对外经贸实务, 2020 (5): 32-35.

[38] 宋津睿, 崔日明. 经济制度差异与中国服务贸易出口竞争力研究 [J]. 对外经贸实务, 2021 (11): 31-35.

[39] 苏杭. 跨境电商物流管理 [M]. 北京: 对外经济贸易大学出版社, 2017.

[40] 唐红涛, 朱梦琦. 贸易距离与跨境电商: 文献综述和展望 [J]. 兰州财经大学学报, 2021, 37 (6): 23-35.

[41] 陶正. 跨境电商企业使用海外仓面临的问题及对策研究 [J]. 物流科技, 2021 (11): 66-68.

[42] 田青, 李桂娥. 跨境电商物流联盟模式运作的优化路径探讨 [J]. 价格月刊, 2021 (6): 88-94.

［43］田宇，朱道立．物流联盟形成机理研究［J］．物流技术，2000（2）：34－36．

［44］王立鹤，宋丽妮，韩媛媛．我国"跨境电商＋海外仓"商业模式研究—基于核心能力建设的技术路径［J］．全球化，2022（6）：56－63．

［45］王晓煜，王泳，白宗宸．"双碳"目标下我国对外贸易的挑战和应对策略［J］．对外经贸实务，2021（10）：8－12．

［46］王宇楠．供应链稳定视角下跨境电商与物流融合发展路径研究［J］．商业经济研究，2022（6）107－110．

［47］项姬秀．跨境电商与物流链的融合发展：基于产业结构优化视角［J］．商业经济研究，2021（24）：108－110．

［48］肖亮，余福茂，杨林霞．目的国网络嵌入、本土化服务能力与跨境B2C出口企业绩效：海外仓策略的一个理论解释［J］．商业经济与管理，2019（1）：5－15．

［49］谢桂梅．跨境电商物流和供应链发展中的机遇、挑战和思考［J］．中国科技投资，2022（12）：1－3．

［50］谢嘉豪．海外仓建设发展存在的问题及对策［J］．北方经贸，2022（11）：16－19．

［51］谢泗薪，尹冰洁．中美贸易摩擦下跨境电商物流联盟风险预判与战略突围［J］．中国流通经济，2019，33（02）：73－82．

［52］熊俊，朱思怡．跨境电商海外仓内部管理优化研究：以北京凯博锦程经贸有限公司为例［J］．对外经贸实务，2021（9）：79－84．

［53］熊励，叶凯雯．跨境电子商务生态发展与政策组合维度的关联性研究［J］．软科学，2020，34（2）：129－136．

［54］薛磊，王丹，张喆．基于供应链的传统国际货代向跨境电商物流转型［J］．物流技术，2022，41（10）：14－18，22．

［55］薛晓芳，李雪，等．跨境电商物流服务能力对顾客价值的影响研究［J］．商业经济研究，2017：79－81．

［56］杨继军，艾玮炜，范兆娟．数字经济赋能全球产业链供应链分工的场景、治理与应对［J］．发展战略研究，2022（09）：49－58．

［57］杨洁．多措并举支持海外仓发展［J］．中国外汇，2022（06）：22－24．

［58］杨子，朱鹏颐，王盛．跨境电子商务物流运输的影响因素及对策创新［J］．科技和产业，2018，18（2）：32－37．

［59］张铎，曹武军．中国对外贸易跨境电商物流的模式分类与风险评价：基于模糊层次分析的实证研究［J］．河南师范大学学报（哲学社会科学版），2019（5）：

53－59.

［60］张薇．平台战略视角下我国跨境电商生态圈布局规划［J］．商业经济研究，2016
（18）：87－88.

［61］张夏恒，郭海玲．跨境电商与跨境物流协同：机理与路径［J］．中国流通经济，
2016（11）：83－92.

［62］张夏恒，张荣刚．跨境电商与跨境物流复合系统协同模型构建与应用研究［J］．
管理世界，2018，34（12）：190－191.

［63］张夏恒．京东：构建跨境电商生态系统［J］．企业管理，2016（11）：102－104.

［64］张颖川．"新常态"下的物流生态系统建设［J］．物流技术与应用，2015，20
（11）：52－57.

［65］张赠富．我国跨境电商海外仓综合服务能力统计测度——基于 TOPSIS 方法［J］．
商业经济研究，2021（21）：103－106.

［66］赵广华．破解跨境电子商务物流难的新思路：第四方物流［J］．中国经贸导刊，
2014（26）：16－20.

［67］赵昕东．新形势下跨境电商业务的物流风险及防范［J］．中国物流与采购，2022
（12）：47－48.

［68］郑小雪，李登峰，王莹．我国出口跨境电商的物流风险评估［J］．商业经济研
究，2016（23）：68－69.

［69］周广澜，范志颖．系统动力学视角下海外仓对跨境电商出口影响［J］．杭州电子
科技大学学报（社会科学版），2021（2）：22－28.

［70］周敏，黄福华．物联网条件下的共同物流运作风险合理分担模型改进［J］．系统
工程，2013，31（1）：111－115.

［71］朱耿，朱占峰，朱一青．人工智能背景下跨境电商物流体系构建的理论和案例剖
析［J］．物流工程与管理，2018（11）：31－35.